classic
Chicken
recipes

classic
Chicken
recipes

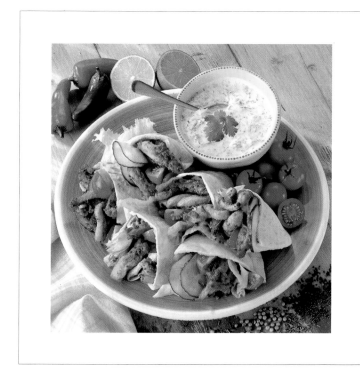

Sue Ashworth	Kathryn Hawkins
Jacqueline Bellefontaine	Cara Hobday
Jennie Berresford	Deh-ta Hsiung
Joanna Craig	Wendy Lee
Jill Eggleton	Louise Steele
Nicola Fowler	Rosemary Wadey
Carole Handslip	Pamela Westland
Jane Hartshorn	

This edition published by Parragon 1999
Mustard is an imprint of Parragon
Parragon
Queen Street House
4 Queen Street
Bath BA1 1HE, UK

ISBN: 0-75253-158-1 (Hardback)
ISBN: 1-84164-396-3 (Paperback)

Printed in Singapore

Edited, designed and produced by Haldane Mason, London

Acknowledgements

Editor: Anne Hildyard

Design: dap ltd

Photographer: St John Asprey (for pages 22, 23–24, 26–31, 33–36, 40, 59–65,
66–73, 78–80, 81–82, 83–86, 87–97, 98, 101–101, 118–125, 127–133, 145, 146–149, 150–155,
156–165, 172–176, 177–185, 186–187, 206–219, 221, 236–247, 248–251)

Home Economist: Jacqueline Bellefontaine (*for above pages*)

Other Photography: Karl Adamson, Sue Atkinson, Iain Bagwell, Martin Brigdale,
Amanda Heywood, Joff Lee, Patrick McLeavey, Clive Streeter

Home Economists: Sue Ashworth, Jennie Berresford, Joanna Craig, Jill Eggleton,
Nicola Fowler, Carole Handslip, Jane Hartshorn, Kathryn Hawkins, Cara Hobday,
Deh-ta Hsiung, Wendy Lee, Louise Steele, Rosemary Wadey, Pamela Westland

The publishers would like to thank the British Chicken Information Service for providing
the recipes on pages 22, 40, 59–65, 81–82, 87–97, 100–101, 127–133, 146–149,
156–165, 172–176, 186–187, 206–219, 221, 236–247.

Recipes on the following pages courtesy of Tom Bridge: 23–24, 26–31, 33–36,
66–73, 78–80, 83–86, 98, 118–125, 145, 150–155, 177–185, 248–251

The publishers would like to thank Divertimenti for kindly loaning them equipment
for the following pages: 64, 80, 82, 87, 89, 91, 101, 124, 128, 129, 130, 145,
159, 160, 161, 173, 213, 216, 217, 218, 236, 241

Note

Cup measurements in this book are for American cups.
Tablespoons are assumed to be 15 ml. Unless otherwise stated, milk is assumed to be
full-fat, eggs are medium and pepper is freshly ground black pepper.

Contents

Pies, Pastries & Terrines 166

Barbecues & Grills 188

Hot & Spicy 222

Introduction

Chicken has become justly popular around the whole world and plays an important part in the modern diet, being reasonably priced and nutritionally sound. It was not always the case, at one time only the affluent could afford to eat chicken. It was not until after World War II, when modern production methods started, that chicken became more plentiful and cheaper, enabling everyone to take advantage of a low-cost, healthy food.

Chicken is a versatile meat that lends itself to an enormous range of recipes, cooking methods and cuisines. Its unassertive flavour means that it is equally suited to cooking with herbs, spices, fruit, vegetables, and sweet and savoury flavours. Because it has a low fat content, especially without the skin, it is an ideal meat for low cholesterol and calorie-controlled diets – 105 grams/3½ ounces of white meat contains only 4 grams of fat. If you want to reduce fat further, cooking methods that require little added fat include poaching, grilling (broiling), roasting or stir-frying. The skin can be left on during cooking to keep the meat moist

and then removed before serving to reduce the fat content. As well as being an excellent source of protein, chicken contains valuable minerals, such as potassium and phosphorus, and some of the B vitamins.

There are many different types of chicken available. Whole birds come as broilers or roasters, boilers, which are older birds that need longer cooking, and small baby chickens, known as poussins. Broilers are also sold jointed into portions. Further options to choose from concern feeding and rearing methods. These include corn or maize-fed chickens, free-range chickens that are not reared intensively but are free to roam in a traditional farmyard and Poulet de Bresse, a French breed that is larger than normal.

The recipes in this book encompass several cooking methods and are gathered from many different cuisines. Choose from soups, starters, snacks and salads, roasts and bakes, casseroles, quick chicken dishes, pies, pastries and terrines, barbecues and grills, and hot and spicy dishes. As well as all the classic dishes, there are creative, contemporary recipes with some surprising twists. Whatever the occasion, the perfect dish is guaranteed to be found in this book.

Buying Guide

When buying fresh chicken, always check the sell-by date and make sure that the chicken feels chilled. Look for chicken that is undamaged, with no dark patches and few traces of feathers. Check the smell, which should be clean and fresh. Remove any giblets and store these separately. The flesh should feel soft and flexible and give slightly when pressed.

CHOOSING A CHICKEN

Baby chicken Also known as poussin or Cornish game hen, these are 4–6-week old birds weighing between 350–625 grams/12–20 ounces. One whole bird is usually needed for each person. Because they are so young and have not developed a lot of flavour, flavour must be added in the form of stuffing or a marinade.

Boiling fowl These are large birds over 10 months old, with a good flavour. They are ideal for casseroles or for making stock, but are generally too tough for roasting or grilling (broiling).

Broiler or frying chicken These birds are reared to produce tender flesh, and are usually 6–8 weeks old, weighing 1.5–2 kg/3–4lb. They are best used jointed and grilled (broiled) or fried, but whole birds can also be roasted, steamed or casseroled.

Capon These are large, castrated cockerels, about 10 weeks old, and can weigh as much as 5 kg/10 lb. They have a greater proportion of white meat and the flesh is delicately marbled with fat which gives it an excellent flavour. In the UK, it is illegal to produce capons.

Corn-or maize-fed chicken These are reared on a diet containing large amounts of corn, a food often used in south-west France. The corn is thought to give a good flavour and the skin of these birds is a distinctive yellow colour. They usually weigh between 1.5–2.25 kg/3–5 lb.

Free-range chicken These have the freedom to feed at will and the space to run free, either in large, airy barns or in the farmyard. Barn-reared birds are slaughtered at 8–10 weeks, and farmyard birds at 1–12 weeks. They have a bigger, broader shape than the factory-reared broiler or roaster, and usually have a better flavour.

Poulet de Bresse Reared in the Burgundy region of France, these birds are fed on natural, high-quality food in free-range conditions. Perhaps because of this, their flavour is believed to be superior and this is reflected in their price.

Roaster These weigh about 1.8–3.5 kg/4–8 lb and are about 10 weeks old when slaughtered. They are best roasted whole, but if they are not too large, they can be jointed and used for frying or grilling (broiling).

Spring chicken Also known as a double poussin, this is a 9–12-week-old bird, weighing about 1.25 kg/2½ lb, which is large enough to feed two people.

Chicken Cuts

When you do not require a whole chicken, various choices of chicken cuts are available ready-packaged. Using cuts means quicker cooking and no wastage. There are choices of preparation as some chicken pieces are skinless and boneless while others have both bone and skin. Of course, the more preparation that is done, the more expensive the cut will be.

Breast
Chicken breasts are available with or without skin and either boneless or with the bone left in. The white meat is lean and succulent and can be simply cooked in butter or oil, or stuffed to add extra flavour.

Leg
The leg can be easily separated into a drumstick and thigh. If left as one piece, a large cut such as this is best poached or casseroled rather than grilled or fried.

Drumstick
This cut is convenient to eat at barbecues or buffet meals as it can be picked up easily. It is ideal for frying or barbecuing and can be first marinated or coated in breadcrumbs.

Thigh
Any slow-cooking method is suitable for this cut, and it is good used in recipes for casseroles and stews. The meat on thighs is dark but it is very succulent and juicy.

Wing
Although not very meaty, many people enjoy this cut when fried or roasted. If the wing tips are cut off, wings are a good candidate for the barbecue (grill).

Minced (ground) chicken
Where a mild flavour is preferred, minced chicken makes a good substitute for minced (ground) red meat. It is also useful to make patties, rissoles and sausages.

Chicken liver
This is found either in the freezer or delicatessen. It is very tasty in rice dishes and can be used to make pâtés or cooked and tossed over warm salads.

Preparation Techniques

There are a number of different ways of preparing a whole chicken for cooking. The following techniques will help to make carving easier, speed up cooking times and even help to save you some money!

Spatchcocking

The spatchcocking technique involves flattening the bird so that it can be cooked more quickly. This method is ideal for grilling (broiling) or barbecuing.

1 Put the chicken on a chopping board with the breast downwards. Cut through the bottom part of the carcass using poultry shears or heavy kitchen scissors, making sure not to cut right through to the breast bone below.

2 Rinse the chicken with cold water, drain and place on a board with the skin side uppermost. Press the chicken flat, then cut off the leg ends. Thread two long wooden skewers through the bird to keep it flat.

Jointing a Chicken

Jointing a chicken yourself is a cheaper option than buying ready-prepared portions and you can choose whether to cut the chicken into four or eight portions. Use either poultry shears or a sharp knife and strong kitchen scissors. First remove the legs: use a sharp knife and cut through the skin where the leg is attached to the body. Hold the leg away from the body and twist to break the ball and socket joint. Cut through the joint and remove the leg. Remove the other leg in the same way. Separate the breast from the back-bone, cut through the flap of skin below the rib cage and cut towards the neck. Pull the breast and back apart and cut through the joints that connect them. Take one side of the breast in each hand and hold skin side down. Bend each side until the breastbone becomes free. Remove it with your fingers and a knife. Cut the breast in half through the wishbone. Now cut each breast in half so that some is included with each wing. Finally, separate the thigh and drumstick.

Boning a Chicken

To make carving simpler, it is necessary to bone a chicken. Use a sharp knife with a short blade and keep the knife against the bone, using short, scraping actions.

1 Dislocate each leg by breaking it at the thigh joint. Carefully remove the wishbone with the small knife.

2 With the bird breast-side down on a chopping board, cut down the centre of the backbone from the neck to the tail end.

3 Working from the front to the back, scrape away the flesh on one side of the backbone, cutting into the bird to expose the ribcage.

4 Repeat on the other side, being careful not to pierce the breast skin with the knife. Pull the rib and backbone from the flesh of the bird.

5 Scrape away the flesh from each thigh bone and cut away the bone at the joint with the small knife or poultry shears. Scrape all the flesh away from the wings up to the first joint.

6 Remove the exposed wing bone by cutting away the rest of the wing at the joint. Cut away the tendon from each fillet and breast. The chicken is now ready for stuffing and rolling.

Cooking Methods for Chicken

All types of chicken can be roasted, from baby chickens to larger birds. With crisp, golden-brown skin and moist, succulent meat, a perfectly roasted chicken is always popular.

ROASTING

Before roasting, remove any fat from the body cavity. Rinse the bird inside and out with water, then pat dry with paper towels. Season the cavity generously with salt and pepper and add stuffing, herbs or lemon if wished. Spread the breast of the chicken with softened butter or oil. Set on a rack in a roasting tin (pan) or shallow baking dish. Roast the bird, and baste two or three times with the pan juices during roasting.

Alternatively, cover the chicken with a piece of muslin (cheesecloth) that has been dipped in melted butter and there is no need to baste. If the chicken is browning too quickly, cover it with foil. Test for doneness by using a meat thermometer or insert a skewer into the thickest part of the thigh. If the chicken is cooked, the juices will run clear with no trace of pink. Put the bird on a carving board and leave to rest for at least 15 minutes before serving. Make a sauce or gravy from the juices left in the roasting tin (pan).

Carving a Chicken

1 Grasp the leg and move it outwards from the body. Using a sharp knife, cut each drumstick and thigh from the body then cut through the joint to separate the drumstick and thigh.

2 Make a deep horizontal cut just above the wing, through the breast, until the knife touches the breastbone.

3 Slice the breast thinly in a series of vertical cuts going down to the first horizontal cut.

CHICKEN ROASTING TIMES

TYPE OF CHICKEN & TEMPERATURE	WEIGHT	COOKING TIME
Poussin 180°C/350°F/Gas Mark 4	500–750 g/1–1½ lb	1–1¼ hours
Chicken 190°C/375°F/Gas Mark 5	1.25–1.5 kg/2½–3 lb	1–1¼ hours
	1.75–2 kg/3½–4 lb	1¼–2 hours
	2.25–2.5 kg/4½–5 lb	1½–2 hours
	2.5–3 kg/5–6 lb	1¾–2¼ hours

GRILLING (BROILING)

Grilling (broiling) is a good way of cooking chicken. The intense heat of the grill (broiler) quickly seals the succulent flesh beneath a crisp, golden exterior. For the best results the chicken should be placed 10–15 cm/4–6 inches away from a moderate heat source. If the chicken seems to be browning too quickly, turn down the heat slightly. If the chicken is grilled (broiled) at too high a temperature too near to the heat, the outside will burn before the inside is cooked. If it is cooked for too long under a low heat, it will dry out. Baby chickens (poussin), spring chickens and small roasters are least likely to dry out and become tough. So that it can brown and cook evenly, cut a whole chicken into joints.

For small chickens, split the chicken on either side of the backbone and cut the backbone out, then with the bird breast-side up, press firmly on the breastbone to break it and flatten the breast. Fold the wing tips back and behind and thread a long metal skewer through one wing, then the breast and out through the other wing. Thread another skewer through the thighs. This technique is known as spatchcocking. Chicken quarters are best reduced to smaller cuts. Divide leg portions into thighs and drumsticks. Breast meat, if cooked in one piece, can be rather dry and is best divided into bite-sized chunks for kebabs (kabobs), or sliced and pounded flat to make escalopes. Wings are perfect for speedy grilling (broiling) – the bones disperse the heat and the skin traps moisture to make a wonderfully succulent, tasty dish.

GRILLING TIMES FOR CHICKEN

TYPE OF CHICKEN	COOKING TIME
Chicken portions	30–35 minutes
Skinless, boneless chicken breast	10–12 minutes
Spring chicken, spatchcocked	25–30 minutes
Poussin, spatchcocked	20–25 minutes
Roasting chicken, halved or spatchcocked	30–40 minutes

Marinades

- Chicken in Pitta Bread *(see page 54)*
- Supreme of Chicken with Black Cherries *(see page 83)*
- Honeyed Citrus Chicken *(see page 97)*
- Golden Glazed Chicken *(see page 159)*
- Chicken in Spicy Yogurt *(see page 192)*
- Mediterranean Grilled Chicken *(see page 194)*
- Tandoori Chicken *(see page 196)*
- Jerk Chicken *(see page 200)*
- Thai Chicken with Peanut Sauce *(see page 202)*
- Sweet and Sour Drumsticks *(see page 221)*

FRYING

This cooking method is suitable for small thighs, drumsticks and joints. To pan-fry, first dry the chicken pieces with kitchen paper so that they brown properly and to prevent spitting during cooking. If required, the chicken can be coated in seasoned flour, egg and breadcrumbs or a batter. Heat oil or a mixture of oil and butter in a heavy frying pan (skillet). When the oil is very hot, add the chicken pieces, skin-side down. Fry until deep golden brown all over, turning the pieces frequently during cooking. The breast usually cooks before the drumsticks and thighs. Drain well on kitchen paper before serving.

SAUTEEING

This method is ideal for small pieces or small birds such as baby chickens. It can combine braising, where the chicken is first sautéed then cooked in stock or other liquid. Heat a little oil or a mixture of oil and butter in a heavy frying pan (skillet). Add the chicken and fry over a moderate heat until golden brown, turning often during cooking to brown all over. Add stock or other liquid, bring to the boil, then cover and reduce the heat. Cook gently until the chicken is cooked through.

STIR-FRYING

Skinless, boneless chicken is cut into pieces of equal size, either strips, small cubes or thin slices. This ensures that the meat cooks evenly and stays succulent. Preheat a wok or saucepan before adding a small amount of oil. When the oil starts to smoke, add the chicken pieces and stir-fry with your chosen flavourings for 3–4 minutes until cooked through. Other ingredients can be cooked at the same time, or the chicken can be cooked by itself, then removed from the pan while you stir-fry the remaining ingredients. Return the chicken to the pan briefly when the other ingredients are cooked.

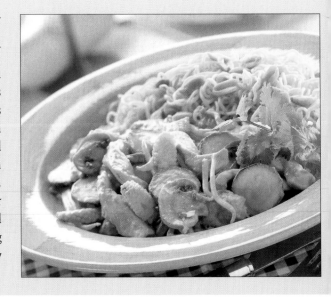

CASSEROLING

Casseroling is a method that is good for cooking joints from larger, more mature chickens, although smaller chickens can be cooked whole. The slow cooking produces tender meat with a good flavour. Brown the chicken in butter or hot oil or a mixture of both. Add some stock, wine or a mixture of both with seasonings and herbs, cover and cook on top of the stove or in the oven until the chicken is tender. Add a selection of lightly sautéed vegetables about halfway through the cooking time.

BRAISING

This method does not require liquid – the chicken pieces or a small whole chicken and vegetables are cooked together slowly in a low oven. Heat some oil in an ovenproof, flameproof casserole and gently fry the chicken until golden all over. Remove the chicken and fry a selection of vegetables until they are almost tender. Replace the chicken, cover tightly and cook very gently on the top of the stove or in a low oven until the chicken and vegetables are tender.

POACHING

Poaching is a gentle cooking method that produces tender chicken and a stock that can be used to make a sauce to serve with the chicken. Put a whole chicken, a bouquet garni, a leek, a carrot and an onion in a large flameproof casserole. Cover with water, season and bring to the boil. Cover and simmer for 1½–2 hours until the chicken is tender. Lift the chicken out, discard the bouquet garni and use the stock to make a sauce. The vegetables can be blended to thicken the stock and served with the chicken.

Food Safety & Tips

Chicken is liable to be contaminated by salmonella bacteria, which can cause severe food poisoning. When storing, handling and preparing poultry, certain precautions must be observed to prevent the possibility of food poisoning.

- Check the sell-by date and best before date. After buying, take the chicken home quickly, preferably in a freezer bag or cool box.

- Return frozen birds immediately to the freezer.

- If storing in the refrigerator, remove the wrappings and store any giblets separately. Place the chicken in a shallow dish to catch drips. Cover loosely with foil and store on the bottom shelf of the refrigerator for no more than two or three days, depending on the best before date. Avoid any contact between raw chicken and cooked food during storage and preparation. Wash your hands after handling raw chicken.

- Prepare raw chicken on a chopping board that can be easily cleaned and bleached, such as a non-porous, plastic board.

- Check the temperature of the refrigerator regularly, it should not exceed 4°C/42°F.

- Frozen birds should be defrosted before cooking. If time permits, defrost for about 36 hours in the refrigerator, or thaw for about 12 hours in a cool place. Bacteria breed in warm food at room temperature and when chicken is thawing. Cooking at high temperatures kills bacteria. There should be no ice crystals and the flesh should feel soft and flexible. Cook as soon as possible after thawing.

- Make sure that chicken is thoroughly cooked. Test for doneness using a meat thermometer – the thigh should reach at least 79°C/175°F when cooked – or pierce the thickest part of a thigh with a skewer, the juices should run clear, not pink or red. Never partially cook chicken with the intention of completing cooking later. Bacteria multiply at an alarming rate, particularly in warm food or during thawing, when optimum conditions prevail for the bacteria to increase.

Chicken Stock

Chicken stock is usually made from a whole bird or wings, backs and legs. This makes a well-flavoured stock. However it can also be made using chicken bones and carcass cooked with vegetables and flavourings. Although it will not be so rich in flavour it is still superior to stock made from a stock cube. Home-made stock can be stored in the freezer for up to six months. A simple chicken stock can be made using the giblets (except the liver which is bitter) with a bouquet garni, onion, carrot and some peppercorns. Salt is not added as this concentrates in flavour as the stock reduces during cooking. Salt can be added to taste when the stock is used in soups and other dishes.

If a whole bird is used to make the stock, the meat can be used in soups and casseroles.

To make chicken stock: Add the wings, backs or whole chicken to a large stockpot with two quartered onions. Cook until the chicken and onion are evenly browned. Cover with cold water, bring to the boil and skim off any scum that rises to the surface. Add two chopped carrots, two chopped celery sticks, a small bunch of parsley, a few bay leaves, a thyme sprig and a few peppercorns. Partially cover and gently simmer for about 3 hours. Strain the stock into a bowl and cool, then chill. When the stock is completely cold, remove the fat that will have set on the surface.

Stuffings for Chicken

- **Springtime Roast Chicken**
  (see page 87)
- **Chicken with Marmalade Stuffing**
  (see page 89)
- **Pollo Catalan** *(see page 90)*
- **Festive Apple Chicken** *(see page 93)*
- **Traditional Roast Chicken** *(see page 99)*
- **Golden Chicken with Mango & Cranberries** *(see page 100)*

Tips for Reducing Fat without Losing Flavour

- Roast whole chickens with their skin, but remove the skin before serving.
- Use cooking methods that don't require added fat, such as steaming, grilling (broiling), stir-frying, baking and roasting.

Stir-frying: Use just a little oil – once it is hot, it spreads further.

Poaching: Poach chicken in stock with added chopped vegetables. When the chicken is cooked through, purée the vegetables and stock to make a tasty sauce.

Baking: Dip chicken pieces in egg white, then into rolled oats or wholemeal flour before baking *(see page 61)*.

Steaming: Steam chicken over a smoky flavoured tea, such as lapsang souchong.

Grilling: Flavour can be added by first marinating the chicken. On the grill (broiler), fat drips away.

- Make gravy with the meat juices, after skimming off the fat. Add chicken stock and fresh herbs for flavour.
- Remove the skin from chicken pieces and rub a mixture of crushed garlic, chopped fresh herbs and spices over the chicken before cooking *(see page 78)*.
- Use marinades such as lemon or lime juice, wine and vinegar to add fat-free flavour.
- Add chopped onion or shallots, either sprinkled over chicken pieces, or placed inside a whole chicken.
- Spread skinless whole chicken or chicken pieces with mustard, or a mixture of honey and mustard with a squeeze of lime juice.
- Serve simply grilled (broiled) chicken with fruit or vegetable salsas *(see page 65)*.

Soups

Chicken soup has a long tradition of being comforting and good for us and some cultures even think of it as a cure for all ills. It is certainly satisfying, full of flavour and easy to digest. For the best results, choose a boiling fowl or a large roasting bird, because immature birds sold for frying are not flavourful enough to make a tasty soup. Most chicken soups benefit from

being made from a good homemade chicken stock, although when time is at a premium, a good quality stock cube can be used instead. Every cuisine in the world has its own favourite version of chicken soup and in this section you'll find a selection of recipes from as far afield as Italy, Scotland and China. The recipes are easy to make and will inspire to you make your own variation of this delicious soup.

Thai Chicken Noodle Soup

Quick to make, this hot and spicy soup is hearty and warming. If you like your food really fiery, add a chopped dried or fresh chilli with its seeds.

Serves 4–6

1 sheet of dried egg noodles from a 280 g/9 oz pack
1 tbsp oil
4 skinless, boneless chicken thighs, diced
1 bunch spring onions (scallions), sliced
2 garlic cloves, chopped
2 cm/$\frac{3}{4}$ in piece fresh ginger root, finely chopped
900 ml/1$\frac{1}{2}$ pints/3$\frac{3}{4}$ cups chicken stock
200 ml/7 fl oz/scant 1 cup coconut milk
3 tsp red Thai curry paste
3 tbsp peanut butter
2 tbsp light soy sauce
1 small red (bell) pepper, chopped
60 g/2 oz/$\frac{1}{2}$ cup frozen peas
salt and pepper

3 Add the drained noodles and heat through. Spoon into bowls and serve with a spoon and fork.

COOK'S VARIATION

Green Thai curry paste can be used instead of red curry paste for a less fiery flavour.

1 Put the noodles in a shallow dish and soak in boiling water as the pack directs.

2 Heat the oil in a large saucepan or wok, add the chicken, and fry for 5 minutes, stirring until lightly browned. Add the white part of the spring onions (scallions), the garlic and ginger and fry for 2 minutes, stirring. Add the stock, coconut milk, curry paste, peanut butter and soy sauce. Season. Bring to the boil, stirring, then simmer for 8 minutes, stirring occasionally. Add the red (bell) pepper, peas and green spring onion tops and cook for 2 minutes.

Chicken Consommé

This is a very flavourful soup, especially if you make it from real chicken stock.
Egg shells are used to give a crystal clear appearance.

Serves 8–10

1.75 litres/3 pints/8 cups chicken stock
150 ml/¼ pint/⅔ cup medium sherry
4 egg whites plus egg shells
125 g/4 oz cooked chicken, sliced thinly
salt and pepper

1 Place the chicken stock and sherry in a large saucepan and heat gently for 5 minutes.

2 Add the egg whites and the egg shells to the chicken stock and whisk until the mixture begins to boil.

3 When the mixture boils, remove the pan from the heat and allow the mixture to subside for 10 minutes. Repeat this process three times.

4 This allows the egg white to trap the sediments in the chicken stock to clarify the soup.

5 Let the consommé cool for 5 minutes.

6 Carefully place a piece of fine muslin (cheesecloth) over a clean saucepan. Ladle the soup over the muslin and strain into the saucepan.

7 Repeat this process twice, then gently re-heat the consommé. Season to taste, add the chicken slices to the consommé and serve.

Cream of Chicken Soup

Tarragon adds a delicate aniseed flavour to this tasty soup.
If you can't find tarragon, use parsley for a fresh taste.

Serves 4
60g/2 oz/4 tbsp unsalted butter
1 large onion, peeled and chopped
300 g/10 oz cooked chicken, shredded finely
600 ml/1 pint/2½ cups chicken stock
1 tbsp chopped fresh tarragon
150ml/¼ pint/⅔ cup double (heavy) cream
salt and pepper
fresh tarragon leaves, to garnish

1 Melt the butter in a large saucepan and fry the onion for 3 minutes.

2 Add the cooked chicken to the pan with 300 ml/½ pint/1¼ cups of the chicken stock.

3 Bring the soup to the boil and simmer for 20 minutes. Allow to cool, then liquidize the soup.

4 Add the remainder of the stock and season with salt and pepper.

5 Add the chopped tarragon, pour the soup into a tureen and add a swirl of cream. Garnish with fresh tarragon and serve with deep fried croûtons.

COOK'S VARIATION

If you can't find fresh tarragon, freeze-dried tarragon makes a good substitute. Single (light) cream can be used instead of the double (heavy) cream.

Chicken Wonton Soup

This Chinese-style soup is delicious as a starter
to an oriental meal or as a light meal.

Serves 4–6
FILLING
350 g/12 oz minced (ground) chicken
1 tbsp soy sauce
1 tsp grated, fresh ginger root
1 garlic clove, crushed
2 tsp sherry
2 spring onions (scallions), chopped
1 tsp sesame oil
1 egg white
$\frac{1}{2}$ tsp cornflour (cornstarch)
$\frac{1}{2}$ tsp sugar
about 35 wonton wrappers
SOUP
1.5 litres/$2\frac{1}{2}$ pints/6 cups chicken stock
1 tbsp light soy sauce
1 spring onion (scallion), shredded
1 small carrot, cut into very thin slices

1 Combine all the ingredients for the
filling and mix well.

2 Place a small spoonful of the filling
in the centre of each wonton wrapper.

3 Dampen the edges and gather up
the wonton wrapper to form a small
pouch enclosing the filling.

4 Cook the filled wontons in boiling
water for 1 minute or until they float
to the top.

5 Remove with a slotted spoon. Bring
the chicken stock to the boil.

6 Add the soy sauce, spring onion
(scallion) and carrot. Add the wontons
to the soup and simmer gently for
2 minutes. Serve at once.

COOK'S TIP

Look for wonton wrappers in
Chinese or oriental supermarkets.
Fresh wrappers can be found in the
chilled compartment and they can
be frozen if you wish. Wrap
in clingfilm (plastic wrap)
before freezing.

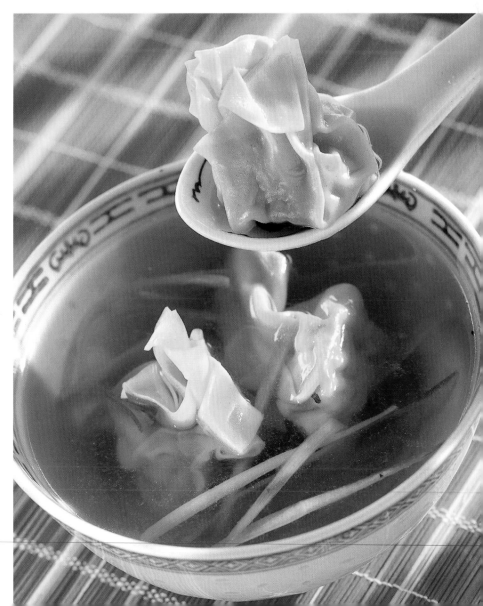

Dickensian Chicken Broth

This soup is made with traditional Scottish ingredients.
It should be left for at least two days before being re-heated,
then served with oatmeal cakes or bread.

Serves 4

60 g/2 oz/$^1/_3$ cup
pre-soaked dried peas

900 g/2 lb diced chicken,
fat removed

1.2 litres/2 pints/5 cups chicken stock

600ml/1 pint/2$^1/_2$ cups water

60 g/2 oz/$^1/_4$ cup barley

1 large carrot, peeled and diced

1 small turnip, peeled and diced

1 large leek, thinly sliced

1 red onion, chopped finely

salt and white pepper

1 Put the peas and chicken into a pan, add the stock and water and bring slowly to the boil.

2 Skim the stock as it boils.

3 When all the scum is removed add the washed barley and salt and simmer for 35 minutes.

4 Add the rest of the ingredients and simmer for 2 hours.

5 Skim and allow the broth to stand for at least 24 hours. Reheat, adjust the seasoning and serve.

COOK'S TIP

Use either whole grain barley or pearl barley. Only the outer husk is removed from whole grain barley and when cooked it has a nutty flavour and a chewy texture.

Tom's Chicken Soup

The potato has been part of the Irish diet for centuries. This recipe is originally from the north of Ireland, in the beautiful area of Moira, County Down.

Serves 4

3 smoked, streaky, rindless bacon slices, chopped
500 g/1 lb boneless chicken, chopped
30 g/1 oz/2 tbsp butter
3 medium potatoes, chopped
3 medium onions, chopped
600 ml/1 pint/2½ cups giblet or chicken stock
600 ml/1 pint/2½ cups milk
150 ml/¼ pint/⅔ cup double (heavy) cream
salt and pepper
2 tbsp chopped fresh parsley, to garnish

1 Gently fry the bacon and chicken in a large saucepan for 10 minutes.

2 Add the butter, potatoes and onions and cook for 15 minutes, stirring all the time.

3 Add the stock and milk, then bring the soup to the boil and simmer for 45 minutes. Season to taste.

4 Blend in the cream and simmer for 5 minutes, garnish with parsley and serve with Irish soda bread.

COOK'S TIP

Soda bread is not made with yeast as bread usually is. Instead it is made with bicarbonate of soda as the raising agent. It can be made with plain (all-purpose) flour or wholemeal (whole wheat) flour.

Chicken & Pea Soup

A hearty soup that is so simple to make yet packed with flavour.
You can use either whole green peas or green or yellow split peas.

Serves 4–6

3 smoked, streaky, rindless bacon
slices, chopped

900 g/2 lb chicken, chopped

1 large onion, chopped

15 g/^{1}/$_2$ oz/1 tbsp butter

500 g/1 lb/2^1/$_2$ cups ready-soaked peas

2.4 litres/4 pints/10 cups chicken stock

150ml/^{1}/$_4$ pint/^{2}/$_3$ cup double (heavy)
cream

2 tbsp chopped fresh parsley

salt and pepper

cheesy croûtes, to garnish

1 Put the bacon, chicken and onion
into a large saucepan with a little
butter and cook over a gentle heat for
8 minutes.

2 Add the peas and the stock to the
pan, bring to the boil, season lightly
with salt and pepper, cover and
simmer for 2 hours.

3 Blend the cream into the soup,
sprinkle with parsley and top with
cheesy croûtes.

COOK'S TIP

Croûtes are slices of French bread
that are fried or baked, then they
can be sprinkled with grated cheese
and lightly toasted.

Chicken, Guinea Fowl & Spaghetti Soup

Guinea fowl has a similar texture to chicken, and although it has a milder flavour than other game, it has a slightly gamier flavour than chicken.

Serves 6
500 g/1 lb skinless chicken, chopped
500 g/1 lb skinless guinea fowl meat
600 ml/1 pint/2¹/₂ cups chicken stock
1 small onion
6 peppercorns
1 tsp cloves
pinch of mace
150 ml/¹/₄ pint/²/₃ cup double (heavy) cream
2 tsp butter
2 tsp plain (all-purpose) flour
125 g/4 oz/1 cup quick-cook spaghetti, broken into short lengths and cooked
pepper
2 tbsp chopped fresh parsley, to garnish

7 Just before serving, add the cooked quick-cook spaghetti.

8 Garnish with parsley and serve.

COOK'S VARIATION

Instead of spaghetti, use small pasta shapes such as ziti or macaroni.

1 Put the chicken and guinea fowl meat into a large saucepan with the chicken stock.

2 Bring to the boil and add the onion, peppercorns, cloves and mace. Simmer gently for about 2 hours until the stock is reduced by one-third.

3 Strain the soup, skim off any fat and remove any bones from the chicken and guinea fowl.

4 Return the soup and meat to a clean saucepan.

5 Add the double (heavy) cream and bring to the boil slowly.

6 To make a roux, melt the butter and stir in the flour until it has a paste-like consistency. Add to the soup, stir until slightly thickened.

Cream of Chicken & Lemon Soup

A refreshing soup with the fresh flavours of lemon
and parsley is perfect on summer days.

Serves 4
60 g/2 oz/4 tbsp butter
8 shallots, sliced thinly
2 medium carrots, sliced thinly
2 stalks celery, sliced thinly
280 g/9 oz skinless chicken breast meat, chopped finely
3 lemons
1.2 litres/2 pints/5 cups chicken stock
150ml/$^1/_4$ pint/ $^2/_3$ cup double (heavy) cream
salt and pepper
sprigs of parsley and lemon slices, to garnish

1 Melt the butter in a large saucepan, add the vegetables and chicken and cook gently for 8 minutes.

2 Thinly pare the lemons and blanch the lemon rind in boiling water for 3 minutes.

3 Squeeze the juice from the lemons.

4 Add the lemon rind and freshly squeezed lemon juice to the pan with the chicken stock.

5 Bring slowly to the boil and simmer for 50 minutes. Cool the soup then blend in a food processor. Return the soup to the saucepan, reheat, season to taste and add the double (heavy) cream. Do not boil at this stage or the soup will curdle.

6 Transfer the soup to a tureen or individual bowls. Serve, garnished with parsley and lemon slices.

Cream of Chicken & Tomato Soup

This soup is very good made wih fresh tomatoes,
but if you prefer, you can use canned tomatoes.

Serves 2
60 g/2 oz/4 tbsp unsalted butter
1 large onion, chopped
500 g/1 lb chicken, shredded very finely
600 ml/1 pint/2½ cups chicken stock
6 medium tomatoes, chopped finely
pinch of bicarbonate of soda (baking soda)
1 tbsp caster (superfine) sugar
150ml/1¼ pint/⅔ cup double (heavy) cream
salt and pepper
fresh basil leaves, to garnish

1 Melt the butter in a large saucepan and fry the onion and shredded chicken for 5 minutes.

2 Add 300 ml/½ pint/1¼ cups chicken stock to the pan, with the tomatoes and bicarbonate of soda.

3 Bring the soup to the boil and simmer for 20 minutes.

4 Allow the soup to cool, then blend the soup in a food processor.

5 Add the remaining chicken stock, season with salt and pepper, then add the sugar.

6 Pour the soup into a tureen and add a swirl of cream. Serve with croûtons and garnish with fresh basil leaves.

Cock-a-Leekie Soup

A traditional Scottish soup in which a whole chicken is cooked with vegetables
to add extra flavour to the stock. Add some of the cooked chicken to
the soup and reserve the remainder for another meal.

Serves 4

1–1.5 kg/2–3 lb oven-ready chicken
plus giblets, if available

1.75–2 litres/3–3¹/₂ pints/8–9 cups
chicken stock

1 onion, sliced thinly

4 leeks, sliced thinly

good pinch of ground allspice
or ground coriander seeds

1 bouquet garni,
(bay leaf, parsley and thyme
sprigs, tied with string)

12 no-soak prunes,
halved and pitted

salt and pepper

warm crusty bread, to serve

1 Put the chicken and giblets, if using, stock and onion in a large saucepan. Bring to the boil and remove any scum from the surface.

2 Add the leeks, allspice or coriander, bouquet garni and salt and pepper. Cover and simmer for 1½ hours until the chicken is falling off the bone.

3 Remove the chicken from the pan and skim any fat from the surface of the soup.

4 Chop some of the chicken flesh and return to the pan. Add the prunes, bring back to the boil and simmer, uncovered, for about 20 minutes.

5 Discard the bouquet garni, adjust the seasoning and serve.

Chicken Mulligatawny Soup

This spicy soup was brought to the west by army
and service personnel returning from India.

Serves 4
60 g/2 oz/4 tbsp butter
1 onion, sliced
1 garlic clove, crushed
500 g/1 lb chicken, diced
60 g/2 oz/¹/₃ cup smoked rindless bacon, diced
1 small turnip, diced
2 carrots, diced
1 small cooking apple, diced
2 tbsp mild curry powder
1 tbsp curry paste
1 tbsp tomato purée (paste)
1 tbsp plain (all-purpose) flour
1.2 litres/2 pints/5 cups chicken stock
150ml/¹/₄ pint/²/₃ cup double (heavy) cream
salt and pepper
1 tsp of chopped fresh coriander (cilantro), to garnish

1 Melt the butter in a large saucepan and cook the onion, garlic, chicken and bacon for 5 minutes.

2 Add the turnip, carrots and apple and cook for a further two minutes.

3 Blend in the curry powder, curry paste and tomato purée (paste), and sprinkle over the flour.

4 Add the chicken stock and bring to the boil, cover and simmer for 1 hour.

5 Liquidize the soup. Reheat, season to taste and gradually blend in the cream. Garnish with coriander and serve over small bowls of boiled or fried rice.

Cream of Chicken & Orange Soup

For a tangy flavour, lemons can be used instead of oranges and the recipe
can be adapted to make duck and orange soup.

Serves 4

60 g/2 oz/4 tbsp butter

8 shallots, sliced thinly

2 medium carrots, sliced thinly

2 sticks (stalks) celery,
sliced thinly

250 g/8 oz skinless chicken breast,
chopped finely

3 oranges

1.2 litres/2 pints/5 cups chicken stock

150 ml/^{1}/$_4$ pint/^{2}/$_3$ cup double
(heavy) cream

salt and white pepper

sprig of parsley and 3 orange slices,
to garnish

1 Melt the butter in a large saucepan,
add the vegetables and chicken meat
and cook gently for 8 minutes.

2 Thinly pare the oranges and blanch
the rind in boiling water for about
3 minutes.

3 Squeeze the juice from the oranges.
Add the orange rind and freshly
squeezed orange juice to the pan with
the chicken stock.

4 Bring slowly to the boil and simmer
for 50 minutes. Cool the soup then
liquidize in a blender or food
processor until smooth.

COOK'S VARIATION

Use 2 small lemons in place of
the oranges. Look for organic or
unwaxed lemons when using rind.

5 Return the soup to the saucepan,
reheat, season to taste and add the
cream. Do not boil at this stage or the
soup will curdle.

6 Transfer the soup to a serving dish
or individual bowls, and serve,
garnished with a sprig of parsley,
orange slices and soda bread.

Chicken Soup with Coriander Dumplings

Use the strained vegetables and chicken to make little patties. Simply mash with
a little butter, shape them into round cakes and fry in butter or oil until golden brown.

Serves 6–8

900 g/2 lb chicken meat, sliced

60 g/2 oz/$^1/_2$ cup plain (all-purpose) flour

125 g/4 oz/$^1/_2$ cup butter

3 tbsp sunflower oil

1 large carrot, chopped

1 stick (stalk) celery, chopped

1 onion, chopped

1 small turnip, chopped

120 ml/4 fl oz/$^1/_2$ cup sherry

3 tbsp sunflower oil

1 tsp thyme

1 bay leaf

1.75 litres/3 pints/8 cups chicken stock

salt and pepper

DUMPLINGS

60 g/2 oz/$^1/_2$ cup self-raising
(self-rising) flour

60 g/2 oz/1 cup fresh breadcrumbs

2 tbsp shredded suet

2 tbsp chopped fresh coriander (cilantro)

2 tbsp finely grated lemon rind

1 egg

salt and pepper

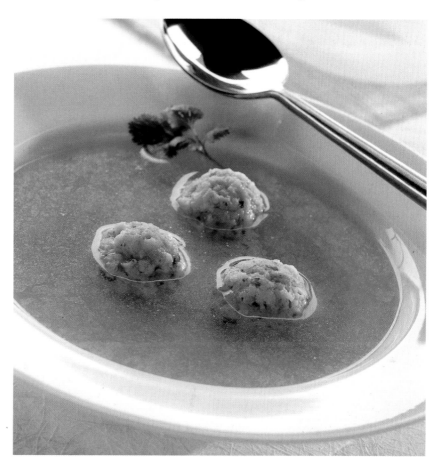

1 Coat the chicken pieces lightly with the flour and season.

2 Melt the butter in a saucepan and fry the chicken pieces until they are lightly browned.

3 Add the oil to the pan and brown the vegetables together. Add the sherry with all the remaining ingredients except the chicken stock.

4 Cook for 10 minutes, then gradually add the chicken stock.

Simmer for three hours, skimming off any excess fat.

5 Strain the liquid into a large clean saucepan and allow to cool.

6 To make the dumplings, mix together all the dry ingredients in a large clean bowl.

7 Add the egg and blend in thoroughly then add enough milk to make a moist dough.

8 Shape the dough into small balls and roll them in a little flour.

9 Cook the dumplings in boiling salted water for 10 minutes.

10 Remove them carefully with a slotted spoon and add them to the soup. Cook for a further 12 minutes, then serve with crusty bread.

Chicken & Leek Soup

This satisfying soup can be served as a main course.
You can add rice and peppers to make it even more hearty, as well as colourful.

Serves 6
30 g/1 oz/2 tbsp butter
350 g/12 oz boneless chicken
350 g/12 oz leeks, cut into
2.5-cm/1-inch pieces
1.2 litres/2 pints/5 cups chicken stock
1 bouquet garni sachet
salt and white pepper
8 pitted prunes, halved
cooked rice and diced peppers
(optional)

1 Melt the butter in a large saucepan, add the chicken and leeks and fry for 8 minutes.

2 Add the stock and bouquet garni sachet, and season well to taste.

3 Bring the soup to the boil and simmer for 45 minutes.

4 Add the prunes with some cooked rice and diced peppers if you wish, and simmer for 20 minutes. Remove the bouquet garni sachet and discard before serving.

COOK'S TIP

Instead of the bouquet garni sachet, you can use a bunch of fresh, mixed herbs, tied together with string. Choose herbs such as parsley, thyme and rosemary.

Chicken & Sweetcorn Soup

A hint of chilli and sherry flavour this chicken and sweetcorn soup,
which has both baby sweetcorn and corn niblets in it,
with red (bell) pepper and tomato for colour and flavour.

Serves 4
1 skinless, boneless chicken breast, about 175 g/6 oz
2 tbsp sunflower oil
2–3 spring onions (scallions), thinly sliced diagonally
1 small or ½ large red (bell) pepper, thinly sliced
1 garlic clove, crushed
125 g/4 oz baby sweetcorn (corn-on-the-cob), thinly sliced
1 litre/1¾ pints/4 cups chicken stock
200 g/7 oz can of sweetcorn niblets, well drained
2 tbsp sherry
2–3 tsp bottled sweet chilli sauce
2–3 tsp cornflour (cornstarch)
2 tomatoes, quartered and deseeded, then sliced
salt and pepper
chopped fresh coriander (cilantro) or parsley, to garnish

1 Cut the chicken breast into 4 strips lengthways, then cut each strip into narrow slices across the grain.

2 Heat the oil in a wok or frying pan, swirling it around until it is really hot. Add the chicken and stir-fry for 3–4 minutes, moving it around the wok until it is well sealed all over and almost cooked through.

3 Add the spring onions (scallions), (bell) pepper and garlic, and stir-fry for 2–3 minutes. Add the sweetcorn and stock and bring to the boil.

4 Add the sweetcorn niblets, sherry, sweet chilli sauce and salt to taste, and simmer for 5 minutes, stirring from time to time.

5 Blend the cornflour (cornstarch) with a little cold water. Add to the soup and bring to the boil, stirring until the sauce is thickened. Add the tomato slices, season to taste and simmer for 1–2 minutes. Serve the soup hot, sprinkled with chopped coriander (cilantro) or parsley.

Chicken Soup with Almonds

This soup can also be made using turkey or pheasant breasts.
Pheasant gives a stronger flavour, particularly if game stock
is made from the carcass and used in the soup.

Serves 4
1 large or 2 small skinless, boneless chicken breasts
1 tbsp sunflower oil
1 carrot, cut into julienne strips
4 spring onions (scallions), thinly sliced diagonally
700 ml/1¹/₄ pints/3 cups chicken stock
finely grated rind of ¹/₂ lemon
45 g/1¹/₂ oz/¹/₃ cup ground almonds
1 tbsp light soy sauce
1 tbsp lemon juice
30 g/1 oz/¹/₂ cup flaked (slivered) almonds, toasted
salt and pepper
bread, to serve

5 Adjust the seasoning, add most of the toasted flaked (slivered) almonds and cook for a further 1–2 minutes.

6 Serve the soup very hot, in individual bowls, sprinkled with the remaining almonds.

COOK'S VARIATION

If you prefer, use finely chopped, skinless toasted hazelnuts in place of the flaked almonds.

1 Cut each breast into four strips lengthways, then slice very thinly across the grain into shreds.

2 Heat the oil in the wok, swirling it around until really hot. Add the chicken and toss it for 3–4 minutes until sealed and almost cooked through. Add the carrot and cook for 2–3 minutes, stirring all the time. Add the spring onions (scallions) and stir.

3 Add the stock to the wok and bring to the boil. Add the lemon rind, ground almonds, soy sauce, lemon juice and plenty of salt and pepper.

4 Bring back to the boil and simmer, uncovered, for 5 minutes, stirring.

Vegetable & Chick-Pea (Garbanzo Bean) Soup

A good tasty soup full of vegetables, chicken and chick-peas (garbanzo beans), with just a hint of spiciness, to serve on any occasion.

Serves 4–6
3 tbsp olive oil
1 large onion, chopped finely
2–3 garlic cloves, crushed
¹/₂–1 red chilli, deseeded and chopped very finely
1 skinless, boneless chicken breast, about 150 g/5 oz, sliced thickly
2 celery sticks (stalks), chopped finely
175 g/6 oz carrots, grated coarsely
1.25 litres/2¹/₄ pints chicken stock
2 bay leaves
¹/₂ tsp dried oregano
¹/₄ tsp ground cinnamon
425 g/14 oz can of chick-peas (garbanzo beans), drained
2 medium tomatoes, peeled, deseeded and chopped
1 tbsp tomato purée (paste)
salt and pepper
chopped fresh coriander (cilantro) or parsley, to garnish
corn or wheat tortillas, to serve

1 Heat the oil in a large saucepan and fry the onion, garlic and chilli very gently until they are softened but not coloured.

2 Add the chicken to the saucepan and continue to cook until well sealed and lightly browned.

3 Add the celery, carrots, stock, bay leaves, oregano, cinnamon, and salt and pepper. Bring to the boil, then cover and simmer gently for about 20 minutes, or until the chicken is tender and cooked throughout.

4 Remove the chicken from the soup and chop it finely, or cut it into narrow strips.

5 Return the chicken to the pan with the chick-peas (garbanzo beans), tomatoes and tomato purée (paste).

Simmer, covered, for a further 15–20 minutes. Discard the bay leaves, then adjust the seasoning.

6 Serve very hot sprinkled with coriander (cilantro) or parsley and accompanied by warmed tortillas.

Chicken & Pasta Broth

This satisfying soup makes a good lunch or supper dish and you can use any vegetables that you have at hand. Children will love the tiny pasta shapes.

Serves 6

350 g/12 oz boneless
chicken breasts

2 tbsp sunflower oil

1 medium onion, diced

250 g/8 oz/1½ cups carrots, diced

250 g/8 oz cauliflower florets

900 ml/1½ pints/3¾ cups
chicken stock

2 tsp dried mixed herbs

125 g/4 oz small pasta shapes

salt and pepper

Parmesan cheese (optional)
and crusty bread, to serve

1 Finely dice the chicken, discarding any skin.

2 Heat the oil and quickly sauté the chicken and vegetables until they are lightly coloured.

3 Stir in the stock and herbs. Bring to the boil and add the pasta. Return to the boil, cover and simmer for 10 minutes. Season to taste and sprinkle with Parmesan cheese, if using. Serve with crusty bread.

COOK'S VARIATION

Broccoli florets can be used to replace the cauliflower florets. Substitute 2 tablespoons chopped fresh mixed herbs for the dried mixed herbs.

Chicken & Chestnut Soup

A rich soup based on a good stock with pieces of chicken and chopped chestnuts for an interesting flavour and texture.

Serves 4–6
2 onions
raw or cooked chicken carcass, chopped, plus trimmings
chicken giblets, if available
1.5 litres/2½ pints/6¼ cups water
1 bouquet garni, (bay leaf, parsley and thyme sprigs, tied with string)
125 g/4 oz/½ cup fresh chestnuts, pierced and roasted for about 5 minutes or boiled for 30–40 minutes, and drained, or 175 g/6 oz/1 cup canned peeled chestnuts
45 g/1½ oz/3 tbsp butter or margarine
45 g/1½ oz/⅓ cup plain (all-purpose) flour
150 ml/¼ pint/⅔ cup milk
1/2 tsp ground coriander seeds
90 g/3 oz/1½ cups carrots, grated coarsely
1 tbsp chopped fresh parsley (optional)
salt and pepper

1 Cut one of the onions into quarters. Put the chicken carcass, giblets, if available, water, the quartered onion and bouquet garni into a saucepan. Bring to the boil, cover and simmer for about 1 hour, stirring occasionally.

2 Strain the stock and reserve 1 litre/1¾ pints/4 cups.

3 Remove 90–125 g/3–4 oz/½–¾ cup of chicken trimmings from the carcass and chop finely. If using canned chestnuts, drain well; if using fresh

chestnuts, peel them. Finely chop the chestnuts. Chop the remaining onion.

4 Melt the butter or margarine in a saucepan and fry the onion gently until soft. Stir in the flour and cook over a low heat for 1–2 minutes.

5 Gradually stir in the reserved stock and bring to the boil, stirring. Simmer

for 2 minutes, then add the milk, coriander, chopped chicken, carrots, chestnuts, and salt and pepper.

6 Bring the soup back to the boil and simmer for 10 minutes, then stir in the parsley, if using. Adjust the seasoning before serving.

Chicken & Sweetcorn Chowder

A quick and satisfying soup, full of flavour and different textures.
Sweetcorn (corn-on-the-cob) is a sweet, juicy addition.

Serves 2

2 tsp oil

15 g/¹/₂ oz/¹/₄ cup
butter or margarine

1 small onion, chopped finely

1 chicken leg, quarter
or 2–3 drumsticks

1 tbsp plain (all-purpose) flour

600 ml/1 pint/2¹/₂ cups
chicken stock

¹/₂ small red, yellow
or orange (bell) pepper,
chopped finely

2 large tomatoes,
peeled and chopped

2 tsp tomato purée (paste)

200 g/7 oz can of sweetcorn (corn-on-
the-cob), drained

generous pinch of dried oregano

¹/₄ tsp ground coriander seeds

salt and pepper

chopped fresh parsley,
to garnish

1 Heat the oil and butter or
margarine in a saucepan and fry the
onion gently until just beginning to
soften. Cut the chicken quarter, if
using, into two pieces. Add the
chicken to the saucepan and fry until
golden brown all over.

2 Add the flour and cook for 1–2
minutes. Then add the stock
gradually, bring to the boil and
simmer for about 5 minutes.

3 Add the (bell) pepper, tomatoes,
tomato purée (paste), sweetcorn,
oregano, coriander, and salt and

pepper. Cover and simmer gently for
about 20 minutes until the chicken is
very tender.

4 Remove the chicken from the soup,
strip the flesh from the bone and chop
it finely with a sharp knife. Then
return the chicken to the soup.

5 Adjust the seasoning and simmer
for a further 2–3 minutes before
sprinkling with chopped, fresh
parsley. Serve the soup very hot with
crusty bread.

Noodles in Soup

Noodles in soup are popular in China. This is a thick, hearty soup, just add more stock if you prefer a thinner soup.

Serves 4
250 g/8 oz cooked, skinless, boneless chicken
3–4 Chinese dried mushrooms, soaked
125 g/4 oz can of sliced bamboo shoots, rinsed and drained
125 g/4 oz spinach, lettuce hearts, or Chinese leaves, shredded
2 spring onions (scallions), finely shredded
250 g/8 oz egg noodles
about 600 ml/1 pint/2$\frac{1}{2}$ cups chicken stock
2 tbsp light soy sauce
2 tbsp vegetable oil
1 tsp salt
$\frac{1}{2}$ tsp sugar
2 tsp Chinese rice wine or dry sherry
a few drops of sesame oil
1 tsp red chilli oil (optional)

1 Cut the meat into thin shreds. Squeeze dry the soaked mushrooms and discard the hard stalk.

2 Thinly shred the mushrooms, bamboo shoots, spinach and spring onions (scallions).

3 Cook the noodles in boiling water according to the instructions on the packet, then drain and rinse under cold water. Place the noodles in a bowl and set aside. Bring the stock to a boil, add about 1 tablespoon soy sauce and pour over the noodles. Keep warm.

4 Heat the oil in a preheated wok or heavy frying pan (skillet), add about half of the spring onions (scallions), the chicken and the vegetables (mushrooms, bamboo shoots and greens). Stir-fry for about 2–3 minutes. Add all the seasonings and blend together well.

5 Pour the mixture into the wok over the noodles, garnish with the remaining spring onions (scallions) and serve immediately.

Hot & Sour Soup

This is one of the most popular soups in Chinese
restaurants throughout the world.

Serves 4
4–6 dried oriental mushrooms (shiitake), soaked
125 g/4 oz cooked chicken or pork
1 cake tofu (bean curd)
60 g/2 oz can of sliced bamboo shoots, drained
1 tbsp cornflour (cornstarch)
600 ml/1 pint/2½ cups chicken stock or water
1 tbsp Chinese rice wine or dry sherry
1 tbsp light soy sauce
2 tbsp rice vinegar
½ tsp ground white pepper
salt
2–3 spring onions (scallions), thinly sliced, to garnish

1 Drain the mushrooms, squeeze dry
and discard the hard stalks. Thinly
slice the mushrooms.

2 Thinly slice the chicken, tofu (bean
curd) and bamboo shoots into narrow
shreds using a cleaver.

3 Mix the cornflour (cornstarch) with
1½ tablespoons of water to form a
paste and set aside.

4 Bring the stock or water to a rolling
boil in a wok or frying pan and add
the mushrooms, chicken, tofu and
bamboo shoots. Bring back to the boil
then simmer for about 1 minute.

5 Add the wine, soy sauce and
vinegar. Bring back to the boil, stirring

in the cornflour (cornstarch) paste.
Add the pepper and season with salt
to taste. Serve hot, sprinkled with the
spring onions (scallions).

COOK'S TIP

Shiitake mushrooms have a
pronounced flavour. Wipe the caps
and stalks before cooking.

Chicken & Noodle One-Pot

Flavoursome chicken and vegetables cooked with Chinese egg noodles in a coconut sauce.
Increase the amount of stock for a thinner soup. Serve the soup in deep bowls.

Serves 4
1 tbsp sunflower oil
1 onion, sliced
1 garlic clove, crushed
2.5 cm/1 inch fresh ginger root, grated
1 bunch spring onions (scallions), sliced diagonally
500 g/1 lb skinless, boneless chicken breasts, cut into bite-sized pieces
2 tbsp mild curry paste
500 ml/16 fl oz/2 cups coconut milk
300 ml/$\frac{1}{2}$ pint/$1\frac{1}{4}$ cups chicken stock
250 g/8 oz Chinese egg noodles
2 tsp lime juice
salt and pepper
sprigs of basil, to garnish

5 Add the lime juice, season to taste and garnish with basil sprigs. Serve at once in deep soup bowls.

COOK'S TIP

Look for canned coconut milk in Asian and oriental supermarkets or in delicatessens.

1 Heat the oil in a wok or large, heavy-based frying pan (skillet). Add the onion, garlic, ginger and spring onions (scallions) and stir-fry for 2 minutes until softened.

2 Add the chicken pieces and curry paste. Stir-fry for about 4 minutes until the vegetables and chicken are golden brown.

3 Stir in the coconut milk, stock and salt and pepper to taste, mixing until well blended. Bring to the boil.

4 Add the noodles to the pan. Cover and simmer for about 6–8 minutes, stirring occasionally until the noodles are just tender.

Starters, Snacks & Salads

Chicken is versatile and quick to cook, making it perfect for innovative and appetizing first courses or light lunches. Its unassertive flavour means that it can be enlivened by exotic fruits and spices and oriental ingredients, such as mirin, sesame oil and fresh ginger root. It is infused with a spicy Middle Eastern flavour after marinating in a rich mixture of spices, then

served in pitta bread with salad and herbed yogurt. There are fritters, classic salads, rarebits, pâtés, potted chicken,

sandwiches, fillings for baked potatoes, and drumsticks that are stuffed and baked, or served with delicious fruity salsas. Because chicken pieces travel well and are easy to eat, many of the recipes are ideal to take on picnics or to pack into a lunch box. The recipes are cosmopolitan, with influences appearing from as far apart as the Mediterranean and Asia.

Oriental Chicken Salad

Mirin, soy sauce and sesame oil give an oriental
flavour to this fresh-tasting salad.

Serves 4
750 g/1½ lb skinless chicken
75 ml/3 fl oz/⅓ cup mirin or sweet sherry
75 ml/3 fl oz/⅓ light soy sauce
1 tbsp sesame oil
3 tbsp olive oil
1 tbsp red wine vinegar
1 tbsp Dijon mustard
250 g/8 oz egg noodles
250 g/8 oz/4 cups bean-sprouts
250 g/8 oz/4 cups Chinese leaves, shredded
2 spring onions (scallions), sliced
125 g/4 oz mushrooms, sliced

1 Pound the chicken pieces out to an even thickness between two sheets of clingfilm (plastic wrap) with a rolling pin or cleaver.

2 Put the chicken in a roasting tin (pan). Combine the mirin and soy sauce and brush the mixture over the chicken. Place in a preheated oven, 200°C/400°F/Gas Mark 6, for 20–30 minutes, basting often. Remove from the oven and allow to cool slightly.

3 Meanwhile, combine the sesame oil, olive oil and vinegar with the Dijon mustard.

4 Cook the noodles according to the packet instructions. Rinse under cold running water, then drain and immediately toss in the dressing.

5 Toss the bean-sprouts, Chinese leaves, spring onions (scallions) and mushrooms with the noodles.

6 Slice the cooked chicken very thinly and stir into the noodles. Serve the salad immediately

Chicken, Papaya & Avocado Salad

Try this recipe with peaches or nectarines instead of papaya.

Serves 4
4 skinless, boneless chicken breasts
1 red chilli, deseeded and chopped
1¹/₂ tbsp red wine vinegar
75 ml/3fl oz/¹/₃ cup olive oil
1 papaya, peeled
1 avocado, peeled
125 g/4 oz alfalfa sprouts
125 g/4 oz bean-sprouts
salt and pepper

1 Poach the chicken breasts in boiling water for 15 minutes or until cooked through. Remove with a slotted spoon and set aside to cool.

2 Combine the chilli, vinegar and oil, season well and set aside.

3 Thinly slice the chicken breasts with a sharp knife.

4 Slice the papaya and avocado to the same thickness as the chicken. Arrange on four plates with the alfalfa sprouts and bean-sprouts. Serve accompanied by the dressing.

COOK'S TIP

If you are using papaya rather than peaches in this recipe, add a little lime juice and grated lime rind to the chilli dressing, for an extra tangy flavour.

Veronica Salad

A delicious salad consisting of strips of cooked chicken with grapes, celery and hard-boiled (hard-cooked) eggs in a lightly curried, minty dressing garnished with chicory (endive).

Serves 6
4 skinless, boneless chicken breasts
2 tbsp olive oil
1 tbsp sunflower oil
1–2 garlic cloves, crushed
1 onion, chopped finely
2 tbsp chopped fresh mint
4 green celery sticks (stalks)
175 g/6 oz/1$\frac{1}{2}$ cups black grapes, preferably seedless
125 g/4 oz/1 cup large white (green) seedless grapes
30 g/1 oz/2 tbsp butter or margarine
1 tbsp plain (all-purpose) flour
$\frac{1}{2}$ tsp curry powder
3 tbsp white wine or stock
5 tbsp milk
2 tbsp natural fromage frais
2 tbsp mayonnaise
1 head chicory (endive)
2 hard-boiled (hard-cooked) eggs, quartered
salt and pepper

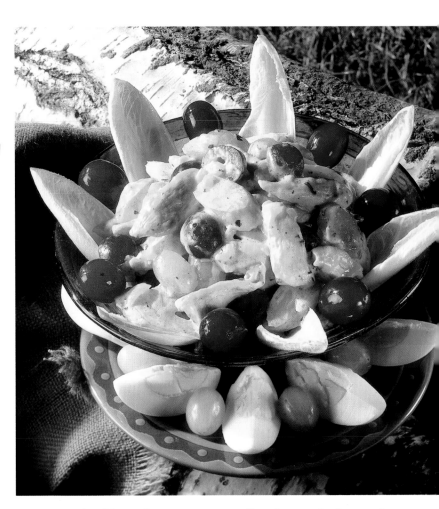

1 Cut the chicken into strips. Heat the oils in a frying pan, add the garlic and chicken, and fry gently until well sealed. Add the onion and fry until the chicken and onion are tender.

2 Stir in the mint and plenty of salt and pepper. Immediately drain off the oil and juices. Put the chicken mixture into a bowl and leave until cold.

3 Cut the celery into thin diagonal slices and add to the chicken.

4 Reserve a few whole black grapes for garnish. If they are large or contain pips (seeds), cut the remainder in half, remove any pips (seeds) and then add to the salad with the white (green) grapes.

5 Melt the butter or margarine in a pan, stir in the flour and curry powder, and cook for 1–2 minutes. Add the wine or stock and the milk, and bring to the boil, simmering until thick. Remove from the heat, season well, and stir in the fromage frais. Cover with clingfilm (plastic wrap) and leave until cold.

6 Stir the mayonnaise into the sauce and add to the chicken mixture. Turn into a serving dish. Arrange the chicory around the edge of the salad with the reserved grapes and hard-boiled (hard-cooked) egg quarters. Cover and chill until ready to serve.

Chicken Pasta Provençale

Use any pasta shape for this salad, but drain thoroughly
so that it does not dilute the dressing.

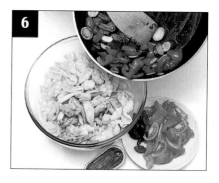

Serves 4
175 g/6 oz dried pasta shapes
4 tbsp French Dressing (see below)
2 tbsp olive oil
350 g/12 oz skinless, boneless chicken breast, cut into strips
2 courgettes (zucchini), sliced
1 red (bell) pepper, deseeded and cut into chunks
2 garlic cloves, sliced
4 tomatoes, cut into wedges
60 g/2 oz can of anchovies, drained and chopped
30 g/1 oz/¼ cup black olives, pitted and halved
sprig of fresh parsley, to garnish
FRENCH DRESSING
3 tbsp olive oil
1 tbsp wine vinegar
1 garlic clove, crushed
½ tsp Dijon or Meaux mustard
1 tsp clear honey
salt and pepper

1 Cook the pasta in boiling salted water for 10–12 minutes until 'al dente'. Drain thoroughly.

2 Whisk all the dressing ingredients together until thoroughly blended.

3 Put the pasta into a bowl with the dressing and mix together.

4 Heat the oil in a frying pan (skillet). Add the chicken and stir-fry for 4–5 minutes, stirring occasionally until cooked, then remove from the pan.

5 Add the courgettes (zucchini), (bell) pepper and garlic to the pan. Fry for 12–15 minutes, stirring, until softened.

6 Add the tomatoes, anchovies and olives to the pasta with the chicken and fried vegetables, and mix thoroughly together.

7 Transfer to a serving dish, garnish with parsley and serve immediately while warm.

Chicken Liver & Watercress Paté

The peppery flavours of the watercress really come through in this soft pâté – try serving it on hot melba toast as a delicious snack

Serves 4–6
60g/2 oz/¼ cup butter
1 onion, chopped
250g/8 oz chicken livers
1 garlic clove, chopped
125g/4 oz watercress, trimmed and chopped
1 tbsp chopped fresh thyme
1 tbsp chopped fresh parsley
1 tbsp sherry
salt and pepper
sprig of watercress, to garnish

1 Heat the butter in a frying pan (skillet) and fry the onion gently for about 5 minutes until soft.

2 Add the chicken livers and garlic and fry gently for 3–4 minutes until cooked through.

3 Set aside to cool slightly, before stirring in the watercress, fresh herbs and sherry.

4 Transfer the mixture to a food processor and process until the chicken livers are finely chopped, but still have some texture – alternatively, put the mixture through a food mill.

5 Transfer the mixture to a serving dish. Cover and leave in the refrigerator to chill. Serve on hot melba toast.

Potted Chicken

Cooked poultry, meat and game can all be prepared in this traditional way:
finely minced (ground) and cooked with onions, spices and sherry or port.
Serve as a first course or sandwich filling.

Serves 4–6

250 g/8 oz boneless
cooked chicken leg meat or any
boneless game, beef or lamb

125 g/4 oz/½ cup butter

1 onion, chopped very finely

1–2 garlic cloves, crushed

2 tbsp sherry or port

about 4 tbsp stock

good pinch of ground mace,
nutmeg or allspice

pinch of dried mixed herbs

salt and pepper

sprigs of fresh thyme, to garnish

TO SERVE

sprigs of watercress

cherry tomatoes
or tomato wedges

crusty bread or fingers of toast

1 Remove any skin and gristle from the poultry, game or meat. Finely mince (grind) twice, or finely chop in a food processor.

2 Melt half the butter in a saucepan and fry the onion and garlic gently until soft but only lightly coloured.

3 Stir the chicken into the pan, followed by the sherry or port and just enough of the stock to moisten the mixture.

4 Season to taste with salt, pepper, mace and herbs. Press the mixture into a lightly greased dish or several small individual dishes and level the top. Cover and chill until firm.

5 Melt the remaining butter and pour a thin layer over the potted chicken. gently press in a few sprigs of thyme and chill thoroughly so that the herbs set in the butter.

6 Serve spooned on to plates, or in individual pots on plates, garnished with watercress, tomatoes and crusty bread or fingers of toast.

Chicken in Pitta Bread

Pitta bread makes a great container for fast and flavoursome meals – either on the move or for a weekend lunch.

Serves 4
1 tbsp cumin seed, crushed
1 tbsp coriander seed, crushed
1 tbsp ground turmeric
1 tbsp black mustard seed
2 tsp chilli flakes
50 ml/2 fl oz/¼ cup olive oil
750 g/1½ lb skinless, boneless chicken thighs
300 ml/½ pt/1¼ cups natural yogurt
90 g/3 oz/3 cups fresh coriander (cilantro)
90 g/3 oz/3 cups fresh mint
juice of 1 lime
salt and pepper

TO SERVE

4 pitta breads
salad leaves (greens)
cucumber slices
tomato wedges
baby tomatoes
sprig of fresh parsley, to garnish

1 Combine the cumin, coriander (cilantro), turmeric, mustard seed, chilli flakes and oil. Season generously with salt and pepper.

2 Cut the chicken into finger width strips and place in a large bowl. Toss in the spice mixture. Leave to marinate for at least 2 hours, or as long as possible.

3 Cook the chicken in a preheated oven, 220°C/425°F/Gas Mark 7, for 15 minutes, turning once or twice.

4 Combine the yogurt and herbs in a food processor until smooth, or finely chop the herbs and stir into the yogurt. Add the lime juice and season well with salt and pepper.

5 To serve, split the pitta breads and warm them through. Stuff generously with salad leaves (greens), cucumber and tomatoes, and divide the chicken strips among them. Spoon over a little yogurt chutney and serve.

Super Club Sandwich

Club sandwiches are intended to be more or less adequate substitutes for
a full meal and can be as many layers high as you can manage!

Serves 1
3 slices white or brown bread
60 g/2 oz/¼ cup butter
125 g/4 oz cooked skinless, boneless chicken, shredded
3 tbsp lemon mayonnaise
4 small crisp lettuce leaves
1 tomato, sliced
5 cm/2 inch piece cucumber, sliced
salt and pepper

TO GARNISH

sprigs of watercress
lemon wedges

1 Toast the slices of bread on both sides until golden, then spread each slice with butter.

2 In a small bowl, mix the chicken with the mayonnaise, and salt and pepper to taste.

3 Cover the first slice of toast with two of the lettuce leaves, then half of the chicken mixture and all of the tomato slices.

4 Cover with the second slice of toast, then the remaining chicken mixture and the sliced cucumber.

5 Place the third slice of toast on top, buttered side down, and press gently to seal.

6 With a sharp knife, cut the whole sandwich into two large triangles or alternatively into quarters, and secure each with a wooden cocktail stick (toothpick), if liked. Serve garnished with sprigs of watercress and lemon wedges.

COOK'S VARIATION

Shredded iceberg lettuce, instead of leaves, adds a crunchy texture.

Spiced Chicken Koftas

Koftas are spicy balls of minced (ground) poultry or meat. In this recipe they are made with chicken, but you could use lamb or beef. Lime pickle is available in Asian food stores and some supermarkets.

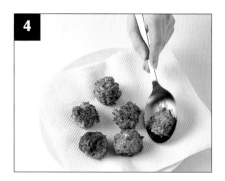

4 Drain on paper towels and serve with lime pickle and lime wedges.

Serves 4

500 g/1 lb skinless, boneless chicken, chopped coarsely

1 garlic clove

2.5 cm/1 inch piece fresh ginger root, grated

$^{1}/_{2}$ green (bell) pepper, deseeded and chopped coarsely

2 fresh green chillies, deseeded and chopped

4 tsp garam masala

$^{1}/_{2}$ tsp ground turmeric

2 tbsp chopped fresh coriander (cilantro)

$^{1}/_{2}$ tsp salt

6 tbsp vegetable oil

lime pickle and lime wedges, to serve

1 Put all the ingredients except the oil and lime pickle into a food processor or blender and process until the mixture is chopped finely. Alternatively, chop the chicken, garlic, ginger, (bell) pepper and chillies very finely, and mix together in a bowl with the garam masala, turmeric, coriander (cilantro) and salt.

2 Shape the mixture between the palms of your hands to form 16 small evenly-shaped balls.

3 Heat the oil in a wok or large frying pan (skillet) and fry the koftas for 8–10 minutes, turning occasionally. If you cannot fit all the koftas into the pan at once, keep the first batch warm in a low oven, while you fry the remaining koftas.

Thai Chicken Spring Rolls

A cucumber dipping sauce tastes perfect with these delicious spring rolls,
filled with chicken and fresh, crunchy vegetables.

Serves 4
1 tbsp light soy sauce
1 tsp sugar
2 tsp cornflour (cornstarch), blended with 2 tbsp cold water
2 tbsp vegetable oil
4 spring onions (scallions), trimmed and sliced very finely
1 carrot, cut into matchstick pieces
1 small green or red (bell) pepper, sliced finely
60 g/2 oz/^{2}/$_3$ cup button mushrooms, sliced
60 g/2 oz/1 cup bean-sprouts
175 g/6 oz/1 cup cooked skinless, boneless chicken, shredded
12 × 20 cm/8 inch spring roll wrappers
oil for deep-frying
salt and pepper
spring onion (scallion) brushes, to garnish

DIPPING SAUCE

50 ml/2 fl oz/^{1}/$_4$ cup light malt vinegar
2 tbsp water
60 g/2 oz/^{1}/$_4$ cup light muscovado sugar
^{1}/$_2$ tsp salt
5 cm/2 inch piece of cucumber, peeled and chopped finely
4 spring onions (scallions), trimmed and sliced finely
1 small red or green chilli, deseeded and chopped very finely

1 Mix together the soy sauce, sugar and cornflour (cornstarch) paste.

2 Heat the oil in a wok or frying pan (skillet) and add the spring onions (scallions), carrot and (bell) pepper. Stir-fry for 2–3 minutes. Add the mushrooms, bean-sprouts and chicken and cook for a further 2 minutes. Season with salt and pepper.

3 Add the cornflour (cornstarch) mixture to the stir-fry and cook, stirring continuously for about 1 minute, until thickened. Leave to cool.

4 Place spoonfuls of the chicken mixture on to the spring roll wrappers. Dampen the edges and roll them up to enclose the filling.

5 To make the dipping sauce, heat the vinegar, water, sugar and salt in a saucepan. Boil for 1 minute. Mix the cucumber, spring onions (scallions) and chilli in a small serving bowl and pour over the vinegar mixture. Cool.

6 Heat the oil and fry the rolls until crisp and golden brown. Drain on paper towels, then serve, garnished with spring onion (scallion) brushes and accompanied by the cucumber dipping sauce.

Chicken Scallops

Served in scallop shells, this dish makes a stylish
presentation for a dinner-party first course.

Serves 4
175 g/6 oz short-cut macaroni, or other short dried pasta shapes
3 tbsp vegetable oil, plus extra for brushing
1 onion, chopped finely
3 slices unsmoked collar or back bacon, derinded and chopped
125 g/4 oz/1½ cups button mushrooms, sliced thinly
175 g/6 oz/¾ cup cooked skinless, boneless chicken, diced
175 ml/6 fl oz/¾ cup crème fraîche
4 tbsp dry breadcrumbs
60 g/2 oz/½ cup mature (sharp) Cheddar, grated
salt and pepper
sprigs of flat-leaf parsley, to garnish

1 Cook the pasta in a large pan of boiling salted water to which you have added 1 tablespoon of the oil. When the pasta is almost tender, drain through a colander, return to the pan and cover.

2 Heat the remaining oil in a pan over medium heat and fry the onion until it is translucent. Add the chopped bacon and mushrooms and cook for a further 3–4 minutes, stirring once or twice.

3 Stir in the drained pasta, diced chicken and the crème fraîche, and season to taste.

4 Brush four large scallop shells with oil. Spoon in the chicken mixture and smooth to make neat mounds.

5 Mix together the breadcrumbs and cheese, and sprinkle over the top of the shells. Press the topping lightly into the chicken mixture, and place under a preheated medium grill (broiler) for 4–5 minutes, until golden brown and bubbling. Garnish with parsley sprigs, and serve hot.

Chicken Pepperonata

All the sunshine colours and flavours of the Mediterranean
are combined in this easy dish.

Serves 4
8 skinless chicken thighs
2 tbsp wholemeal (whole wheat) flour
2 tbsp olive oil
1 small onion, sliced thinly
1 garlic clove, crushed
1 each large red, yellow and green (bell) peppers, sliced thinly
425 g/14 oz can chopped tomatoes
1 tbsp chopped oregano
salt and pepper
fresh oregano, to garnish

1 Remove the skin from the chicken thighs and toss in the flour.

2 Heat the oil in a wide pan and fry the chicken quickly until sealed and lightly browned, then remove from the pan. Add the onion to the pan and gently fry until soft. Add the garlic, (bell) peppers, tomatoes and oregano, then bring to the boil, stirring.

3 Arrange the chicken over the vegetables, season well with salt and pepper, then cover the pan tightly and

simmer for 20–25 minutes or until the chicken is completely cooked through and tender.

4 Season to taste, garnish with oregano and serve with crusty wholemeal (whole wheat) bread.

COOK'S TIP

For extra flavour, halve the peppers and grill (broil) under a preheated grill until the skins are charred. Leave to cool then remove the skins and seeds. Slice the peppers thinly and use in the recipe.

Chicken Pan Bagna

Perfect for a picnic or packed lunch, this Mediterranean-style
sandwich can be prepared ahead.

Serves 6
1 long French stick
1 garlic clove
120 ml/4 floz/$^{1}/_{2}$ cup olive oil
20 g/$^{3}/_{4}$ oz can anchovy fillets
350 g/12 oz cold roast chicken
2 large tomatoes, sliced
8 large, pitted black olives, chopped
pepper

1 Cut the French stick in half
lengthways and open out.

2 Cut the garlic clove in half and rub
over the bread. Sprinkle the cut
surface of the bread with the oil.

3 Drain the anchovies, thinly slice
the chicken and arrange over the
bread with the tomatoes.

4 Scatter with black olives and plenty
of pepper. Sandwich the loaf back
together and wrap tightly in foil until
required. Cut into slices to serve.

COOK'S TIP

Arrange a few fresh basil leaves in
between the tomato slices to add a
warm, spicy flavour. Use a good
quality olive oil in this recipe for
extra flavour.

Oaty Chicken Pieces

A very low-fat chicken recipe with a refreshingly light, mustard-spiced sauce, which is ideal for a healthy lunchbox or a light meal with salad.

Serves 4
30 g/1 oz/¹/₃ cup rolled oats
1 tbsp chopped fresh rosemary
4 skinless chicken quarters
1 egg white
150 g/5 oz/¹/₂ cup natural low-fat fromage frais
2 tsp wholegrain mustard
salt and pepper

1 Mix together the oats, rosemary and salt and pepper.

2 Brush each piece of chicken evenly with egg white, then coat in the oat mixture. Place on a baking sheet and bake in a preheated oven, 200°C/400°F/Gas Mark 6, for about 40 minutes or until the juices run clear when the chicken is pierced.

3 Mix together the fromage frais and mustard, season to taste then serve with the chicken, hot or cold, with a grated carrot salad.

COOK'S VARIATION

Instead of chicken quarters, use skinless, boneless chicken breasts, which are easier to slice. Reduce the cooking time by about 10 minutes and test for doneness.

Chicken & Cheese Jackets

Use the breasts from a roasted chicken for this delicious, healthy snack.

Serves 4
4 large baking potatoes
250 g/8 oz cooked, boneless chicken breasts
4 spring onions (scallions)
250 g/8 oz/1 cup low-fat soft cheese or Quark
pepper

1 Scrub the potatoes and prick them all over with a fork. Bake in a preheated oven, 200°C/400°F/Gas Mark 6, for about 50 minutes until tender, or cook in a microwave on High/100% power for 12–15 minutes.

2 Dice the chicken, trim and thickly slice the spring onions (scallions) and mix with the low-fat soft cheese.

3 Cut a cross through the top of each potato and pull slightly apart. Spoon the chicken filling into the potatoes and sprinkle with pepper. Serve immediately with coleslaw, green salad or a mixed salad.

COOK'S TIP

Look for Quark in the chilled section. It is a low-fat, white, fresh curd cheese made from cow's milk with a delicate, slightly sour flavour.

Cheesy Garlic Drummers

Ideal for informal parties, these tasty chicken drumsticks can be prepared for cooking a day in advance. Instead of baking the chicken drumsticks, you could cook them on the barbecue instead.

Serves 6
15 g/¹/₂ oz/1 tbsp butter
1 garlic clove, crushed
3 tbsp chopped fresh parsley
125 g/4 oz/¹/₂ cup ricotta cheese
4 tbsp grated Parmesan cheese
3 tbsp fresh breadcrumbs
12 chicken drumsticks
salt and pepper
lemon slices, to garnish

1 Melt the butter and fry the garlic gently without browning, stirring for 1 minute.

2 Remove from the heat and stir in the parsley, the cheeses, breadcrumbs and seasoning.

3 Carefully loosen the skin around the chicken drumsticks.

4 Push about a tablespoon of the stuffing under the skin of each drumstick. Arrange the drumsticks in a wide baking tin.

5 Bake in a preheated oven, 190°C/375°F/ Gas Mark 5, for about 45 minutes until golden. Serve hot or cold, garnished with lemon slices.

COOK'S TIP

Any strongly flavoured cheese can be used instead of the Parmesan. Try a matured Cheddar cheese or use another Italian cheese; pecorino.

Old English Spicy Chicken Salad

For this simple, refreshing summer salad you can use leftover roast chicken, or ready-roasted chicken to save time. Add the dressing just before serving, or the spinach will lose its crispness if left in the dressing for too long.

Serves 4
250 g/8 oz young spinach leaves
3 sticks (stalks) celery, sliced thinly
1/2 cucumber, sliced thinly
2 spring onions (scallions), sliced thinly
3 tbsp chopped fresh parsley
350g/12oz boneless, roast chicken, sliced thinly
DRESSING
2.5 cm/1inch piece fresh ginger root, grated finely
3 tbsp olive oil
1 tbsp white wine vinegar
1 tbsp clear honey
1/2 tsp ground cinnamon
salt and pepper
smoked almonds, to garnish (optional)

1 Thoroughly wash and dry the spinach leaves.

2 Toss the celery, cucumber and spring onions (scallions) with the spinach and parsley in a large bowl.

3 Transfer to serving plates and arrange the chicken over the salad.

4 In a screw-topped jar, combine all the dressing ingredients and shake well to mix.

5 Season to taste then pour over the salad. Scatter a few smoked almonds over the salad to garnish, if using.

Sticky Chicken Drummers with Mango Salsa

Delicious served hot or cold, and any leftover chicken can be packed in lunchboxes for a tasty alternative to sandwiches.

Serves 4
8 skinless chicken drumsticks
3 tbsp mango chutney
2 tsp Dijon mustard
2 tsp oil
1 tsp paprika
1 tsp black mustard seeds, roughly crushed
$^1/_2$ tsp turmeric
2 garlic cloves, chopped
salt and pepper
SALSA
1 mango, diced
1 tomato, chopped finely
$^1/_2$ red onion, sliced thinly
2 tbsp chopped fresh coriander (cilantro)

1 Using a small, sharp knife, slash each drumstick three or four times then place in a roasting tin.

2 Mix together the mango chutney, mustard, oil, spices, garlic and salt and pepper and spoon over the chicken drumsticks, turning until they are coated all over with the glaze.

3 Cook in a preheated oven, 200°C/ 400°F/Gas Mark 6, for 40 minutes, brushing with the glaze several times during cooking until the chicken is well browned and the juices run clear when pierced with a skewer.

4 Meanwhile, mix together the mango, tomato, onion and coriander (cilantro) for the mango salsa. Season to taste and chill until needed.

5 Arrange the chicken drumsticks on a serving plate and serve hot or cold with the mango salsa.

COOK'S VARIATION

Use mild curry powder instead of the turmeric.

Solomongundy

This recipe is ideally suited as a cold platter for a buffet party or a
spectacular starter for a special meal.

Serves 4
1 large lettuce
4 chicken breasts, cooked and sliced thinly
8 rollmop herrings and their marinade
6 hard-boiled (hard-cooked) eggs, quartered
125 g/4 oz/^{2}/$_3$ cup cooked ham, sliced
125 g/4 oz/2^2/$_3$ cup roast beef, sliced
125 g/4 oz/^{2}/$_3$ cup roast lamb, sliced
150 g/6 oz/1 cup mangetout, cooked
125 g/4 oz/^{3}/$_4$ cup seedless black grapes,
20 stuffed olives, sliced
12 shallots, boiled
60 g/2 oz/^{1}/$_2$ cup flaked almonds
60 g/2 oz/^{1}/$_3$ cup sultanas (golden raisins)
2 oranges
sprig of mint
salt and pepper

1 Spread out the lettuce leaves on a large oval platter.

2 Arrange the chicken in three sections or lines on the platter.

3 Place the roll mops, eggs and meats in lines or sections over the remainder of the platter.

4 Use the mangetout, grapes, olives, shallots, almonds and sultanas to fill in the spaces between the sections.

5 Grate the rind from the oranges and sprinkle over the whole platter. Peel and slice the oranges and add the orange slices, mint sprig to the platter. Season well with salt and pepper.

6 Finally, sprinkle with the marinade from the herrings and serve with fresh crusty bread.

COOK'S VARIATION

Should you wish, serve with cold, cooked vegetables, such as sliced beans, baby sweetcorn (corn-on-the-cob) and cooked beetroot (beets).

Potted Smoked Chicken

This recipe can be made a few days ahead and kept chilled until needed.
A food processor makes light work of blending the ingredients,
but you can pound by hand for a more coarse mixture.

Serves 4–6

350g/12 oz/2¹/₂ cups
chopped smoked chicken

pinch each of grated nutmeg and mace

125 g/4 oz/¹/₂ cup butter, softened

2 tbsp port

2 tbsp double (heavy) cream

salt and pepper

1 Place the smoked chicken in a large bowl with all the ingredients, and season well.

2 Pound until the mixture is very smooth or blend in a food processor.

3 Transfer the mixture to individual earthenware pots or one large pot.

4 Cover with buttered greaseproof paper and weight down with cans or weights.

5 Chill for 4 hours.

6 Remove the paper and cover with clarified butter (see Cook's Tip).

7 Serve with slices of brown bread and fresh butter.

COOK'S TIP

To make clarified butter:
Place 250 g/8 oz/1 cup butter in a saucepan and heat gently, skimming off the foam as the butter heats. The sediment sinks to the bottom of the pan as the butter heats. When completely melted, remove the pan from the heat and leave it to stand for a least 4 minutes. Strain the butter through a piece of muslin (cheesecloth) into a bowl. Allow the butter to cool a little before pouring it over the surface of the potted chicken.

Chicken & Herb Fritters

These fritters are delicious served with a green salad,
a fresh vegetable salsa or a chilli sauce dip.

Makes 8
500 g/1lb mashed potato, with butter added
250 g/8 oz/1⅓ cups chopped, cooked chicken
125 g/4 oz/⅔ cups cooked ham, chopped finely
1 tbsp mixed herbs
2 eggs, lightly beaten
milk
125 g/4 oz/2 cups fresh brown breadcrumbs
oil for shallow frying
salt and pepper

1 In a large bowl, blend the potatoes, chicken, ham, herbs and 1 egg, and season well.

2 Shape the mixture into small balls or flat pancakes.

3 Add a little milk to the second egg.

4 Place the breadcrumbs on a plate. Dip the balls in the egg and milk mixture then roll in the breadcrumbs, to coat them completely.

5 Heat the cooking oil in a large frying pan (skillet) and cook the fritters until they are golden brown.

COOK'S TIP

A mixture of chopped fresh tarragon and parsley make a fresh and flavourful addition to these fritters.

Chicken Rarebit

A tasty snack that can be served alone as a snack or to accompany a light, clear soup.

Serves 4
250 g/8 oz/2 cups grated Wensleydale
250 g/8 oz/1$\frac{1}{3}$ cups shredded, cooked chicken
1 tbsp butter
1 tbsp Worcestershire sauce
1 tsp dry English mustard
2 tsp plain flour
4 tbsp mild beer
4 slices of bread, toasted on both sides
salt and pepper
1 tbsp chopped fresh parsley, to garnish

1 Place the cheese, chicken, butter, Worcestershire sauce, mustard, flour and beer in a small saucepan. Mix together and season.

2 Gently bring the mixture to the boil and remove from the heat immediately.

3 Beat until the mixture becomes creamy in texture, and allow to cool.

4 Toast the bread and spread with the chicken mixture. Place under a hot grill (broiler) until bubbling and golden brown.

5 Sprinkle with a little parsley and serve with cherry tomatoes.

Open Chicken Sandwiches

These tasty sandwiches are good as a snack on their own or they can be served as part of a spread.

Serves 6

3 hard-boiled (hard-cooked) eggs, the yolk sieved & the white chopped

30 g/1 oz/2 tbsp butter, softened

2 tbsp English mustard

1 tsp anchovy essence

250 g/8 oz/2 cups grated Cheddar cheese

3 cooked, skinless chicken breasts, chopped finely

6 thick slices of bread (crusts removed) or a large french stick cut lengthways, then cut into 6 pieces and buttered

12 slices each of tomato and cucumber

pepper

1 Reserve the yolk and the white from 1 egg.

2 Mix the remaining egg with the butter, mustard and anchovy essence and season well with pepper.

3 Mix in the cheese and chicken and spread the mixture on the bread.

4 Make alternate rows of the egg yolk and the egg white over the chicken mixture. Arrange the tomato and cucumber slices over the egg rows and serve.

COOK'S TIP

If you prefer a less hot flavour, use a milder mustard. Add mayonnaise if wished and garnish with cress.

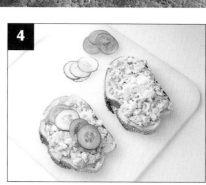

Coronation Chicken

This classic salad is good as a starter or as part of a buffet.
Mango chutney makes a tasty addition.

Serves 6
4 tbsp olive oil
900 g/2lb chicken meat, diced
125 g/4 oz/$^2/_3$ cup rindless, smoked bacon, diced
12 shallots
2 garlic cloves, crushed
1 tbsp mild curry powder
300 ml/$^1/_2$ pint/1$^1/_4$ cups mayonniase
1 tbsp runny honey
1 tbsp chopped fresh parsley
90 g/3 oz/$^1/_2$ cup seedless black grapes, quartered
pepper

1 Heat the oil in a large frying pan add the chicken, bacon, shallots, garlic and curry powder. Cook slowly for about 15 minutes.

2 With a slotted spoon, spoon the mixture into a clean mixing bowl

3 Allow the mixture to cool completely then season well.

4 Blend the mayonnaise with a little honey, then add the parsley.

5 Toss the chicken in the mixture.

6 Place the mixture in a deep serving dish, garnish with the grapes and serve with cold saffron rice.

Chicken with Pear & Blue Cheese Salad

The combination of chicken, blue cheese and pears is delicious in this warm salad.

Serves 6

50 ml/2 fl oz/¼ cup olive oil
6 shallots, sliced
1 garlic clove, crushed
2 tbsp chopped fresh tarragon
1 tbsp English mustard
6 skinless, boneless chicken breasts
1 tbsp flour
150 ml/¼ pint/⅔ cup chicken stock
1 apple, diced finely
1 tbsp chopped walnuts
2 tbsp double (heavy) cream
salt and pepper

SALAD

250 g/8 oz/3½ cups cooked rice
2 large pears, diced
150 g/5 oz/1 cup blue cheese, diced
1 red (bell) pepper, diced
1 tbsp chopped fresh coriander (cilantro)
1 tbsp sesame oil

1 Place the olive oil, shallots, garlic, tarragon and mustard in a deep bowl. Season well and mix the ingredients together thoroughly.

2 Place the chicken in the marinade, cover with cling film (plastic wrap) and chill in the refrigerator for about 4 hours.

3 Drain the chicken, reserving the marinade. Quickly fry the chicken in a large, deep non-stick frying pan for 4 minutes on both sides. Remove the chicken from the pan to a warm serving dish. Meanwhile add the marinade to the pan, bring to the boil and sprinkle with the flour. Add the

chicken stock, apple and walnuts and gently simmer for 5 minutes. Return the chicken to the sauce, add the cream and cook for 2 minutes.

4 Mix the salad ingredients together, place a little on each plate and top with a chicken breast and a spoonful of the sauce.

Waldorf Summer Chicken Salad

This colourful and healthy dish is a variation of a classic salad.

Serves 4
500 g/1lb red apples, diced
3 tbsp fresh lemon juice
150 ml/¼ pint/⅔ cup light mayonnaise
1 head of celery
4 shallots, sliced
1 garlic clove, crushed
90 g/3 oz/¾ cup walnuts, chopped
500 g/1 lb cooked chicken, cubed
1 Cos lettuce
pepper
sliced apple and walnuts, to garnish

1 Place the apples in a bowl with the lemon juice and 1 tablespoon of mayonnaise. Leave for 40 minutes.

2 Slice the celery very thinly.

3 Add the celery with the shallots, garlic and walnuts to the apple, mix and then add the remaining mayonnaise and blend thoroughly.

4 Add the chicken, mix, and line a glass salad bowl or serving dish with the lettuce. Pile the chicken salad into the centre, sprinkle with pepper and garnish with apple slices and walnuts.

COOK'S TIP

Instead of the shallots, use spring onions (scallions) for a milder flavour. Trim the spring onions and slice finely.

Spiced Chicken & Grape Salad

Tender chicken breast, sweet grapes and crisp celery coated in a mild curry
mayonnaise make a wonderful al fresco lunch.

Serves 4

500 g/1 lb cooked skinless,
boneless chicken breasts

2 celery sticks (stalks), sliced finely

250 g/8 oz/2 cups black grapes

60 g/2 oz/¹/₂ cup split almonds,
toasted

pinch of paprika

sprigs of fresh coriander (cilantro)
or flat-leafed parsley, to garnish

CURRY SAUCE

150 ml/¹/₄ pint/¹/₂ cup
mayonnaise

125 g/4 oz/¹/₂ cup natural
fromage frais

1 tbsp clear honey

1 tbsp curry paste

1 Cut the chicken into fairly large
pieces and transfer to a bowl with the
sliced celery.

2 Halve the grapes, remove the seeds
and add to the bowl.

3 To make the curry sauce, mix the
mayonnaise, fromage frais, honey and
curry paste together until blended.

4 Pour the curry sauce over the salad
and mix together carefully until well
coated.

5 Transfer to a shallow serving dish
and sprinkle with the almonds and
paprika. Garnish with the coriander
(cilantro) or parsley.

Crunchy-topped Chicken/Spiced Chicken Salad

Cook four chicken pieces together, and serve two hot, topped with a crunchy herb mixture and white sauce, with potatoes or pasta. Use the remainder for a spicy chicken salad.

Serves 2
4 chicken thighs
oil for brushing
garlic powder
1/2 dessert (eating) apple, grated coarsely
1 1/2 tbsp dry parsley
and thyme stuffing mix
salt and pepper
pasta shapes, to serve

SAUCE
15 g/1/2 oz/1 tbsp butter
2 tsp plain (all-purpose) flour
5 tbsp milk
2 tbsp dry white wine or stock
1/2 tsp dried mustard powder
1 tsp capers or chopped gherkins

SPICED CHICKEN SALAD
1/2 small onion, chopped finely
1 tbsp oil
1 tsp tomato purée (paste)
1/2 tsp curry powder
1 tsp apricot jam
1 tsp lemon juice
2 tbsp mayonnaise
1 tbsp soured cream
90 g/3 oz/3/4 cup seedless grapes, halved

1 Place the chicken in an ovenproof dish. Brush with oil, sprinkle with garlic powder and season. Place in a preheated oven, 200°C/400°F/Gas Mark 6, for 25 minutes.

2 Combine the apple and stuffing mix. Baste the chicken, then spoon the mixture over two of the pieces. Return to the oven for about 10 minutes until the stuffing is browned and the chicken is cooked.

3 To make the sauce, melt the butter in a pan, stir in the flour and cook for 1–2 minutes. Add the milk gradually, then the wine or stock. Bring to the boil. Stir in the mustard and capers or gherkins. Serve the chicken with the sauce and pasta shapes.

4 For the salad, fry the onion gently in the oil until barely coloured. Add the tomato purée, curry powder and jam, and cook for 1 minute. Cool.

5 Blend in a food processor. Beat in the lemon juice, mayonnaise and soured cream. Season to taste.

6 Cut the chicken into strips and add to the sauce with the grapes. Mix and chill. Serve with rice and salad.

Roasts & Bakes

The aroma of roasting chicken is always tempting and in this section there are a wealth of delightful recipes. Traditional roast chicken is included, with all the trimmings, as well as many other imaginative treatments. Unusual stuffings add interest – try courgette (zucchini) and lime, marmalade, or oat and herb stuffing. Many of the recipes in this section exploit the complementary flavours of chicken and fruits and there are some enticing taste combinations including cranberries, mango, black cherries, dried apples, peaches, plums, oranges and mangoes. There are chicken pieces wrapped in bacon, stuffed with ham and cheese, or brushed with honey and mustard. Whole chickens are sprinkled with seeds or cooked with fresh young vegetables. Tasty stuffings are tucked just under the skin to impart flavour and there are boned, easy-to-slice chicken dishes.

Roast Chicken with Coriander & Garlic

This recipe for chicken is coated with a fresh-flavoured marinade then roasted.
Try serving it with rice, yogurt and salad.

Serves 4–6
3 sprigs fresh coriander (cilantro), chopped
4 garlic cloves
1/2 tsp salt
1 tsp pepper
4 tbsp lemon juice
4 tbsp olive oil
1 large chicken
pepper

1 Place the chopped coriander (cilantro), garlic, salt, pepper, lemon juice and olive oil in a pestle and mortar and pound together or blend in a food processor.

2 Chill the mixture for 4 hours to allow the flavour to mature.

3 Place the chicken in a roasting tin (pan). Coat generously with the coriander and garlic mixture.

4 Sprinkle with pepper and roast in a preheated oven, 190°C/375°F/Gas Mark 5, on a low shelf for about 1 1/2 hours, basting every 20 minutes with the coriander mixture. If the chicken starts to look brown, cover with foil.

COOK'S VARIATION

Any fresh herb can be used in this recipe instead of the coriander (cilantro). Tarragon or thyme are a good combination with chicken.

Roast Chicken Breasts with Bacon & Dripping(s) Triangles

Chicken supremes have a little bit of the wing bone left which makes them easy to pick up and eat. In this recipe, a tart, fruity sauce perfectly complements the chicken and dripping(s) triangles.

Serves 8
60 g/2 oz/4 tbsp butter
juice of 1 lemon
250g/8 oz/1 cup redcurrants or cranberries
1–2 tbsp muscavado sugar
8 chicken supremes or breasts
16 slices of streaky bacon
thyme
60 g/2 oz/4 tbsp beef dripping(s)
4 slices of bread, cut into triangles
salt and pepper

1 Heat the butter in a saucepan, add the lemon juice and redcurrants or cranberries, muscavado sugar and salt and pepper. Cook for 1 minute and allow to cool.

2 Meanwhile, season the chicken.

3 Wrap 2 slices of streaky bacon over each breast. Sprinkle with thyme.

4 Wrap each breast in a piece of lightly greased foil and place in a roasting tin (pan). Roast in a preheated oven, 200°C/400°F/Gas Mark 6, for 15 minutes. Remove the foil and roast for another 10 minutes.

5 Heat the dripping(s) in a frying pan and fry the bread triangles on both sides until golden brown.

6 Arrange the triangles on a large serving plate and top each with a chicken breast. Serve with a spoonful of the fruit sauce.

Breast of Chicken with York Ham & Stilton Cheese

Beetroot is one of the most underrated vegetables, adding flavour and colour to numerous dishes. Tender young beetroot are used in this recipe.

Serves 4
4 chicken supremes
8 fresh sage leaves
8 thin slices of York ham
250g/8 oz/2 cups Stilton cheese, cut into 8 slices
8 slices rindless streaky bacon
150 ml/1¼ pint/⅔ cup chicken stock
2 tbsp port
24 shallots
500 g/1 lb baby beetroot, cooked
1 tbsp cornflour, blended with a little port
salt and pepper

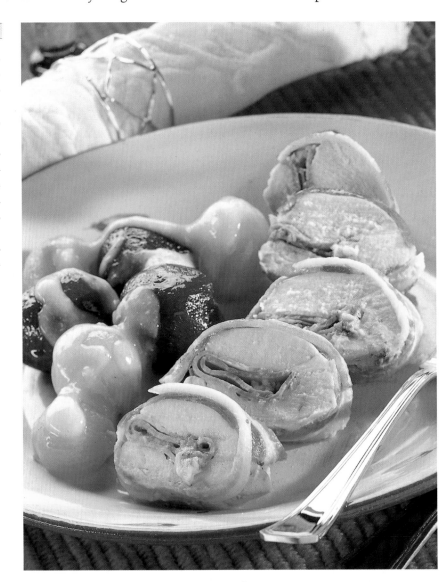

1 Cut a long slit horizontally along each chicken breast to make a pocket.

2 Insert 2 sage leaves into each pocket and season lightly.

3 Wrap each slice of ham around a slice of cheese and place 2 into each chicken pocket.

4 Carefully wrap enough bacon around each breast to completely cover the pockets containing the cheese and ham.

5 Place the breasts in an ovenproof casserole dish and pour over the chicken stock and port.

6 Add the shallots, cover with a lid or cooking foil and braise in a preheated oven, 190°C/375°F/Gas Mark 5, for about 40 minutes.

7 Carefully place each breast onto a cutting board and slice through them to create a fan effect. Serve them on a warm serving dish with the shallots and beetroot.

8 Put the juices from the casserole into a saucepan and bring to the boil, remove from the heat and add the cornflour paste. Gently simmer and cook the sauce for 2 minutes, then pour over the shallots and beetroot.

Pot Roast Orange & Sesame Chicken

This colourful, nutritious pot-roast could be served for a family meal or for a special dinner.
Add more vegetables if you're feeding a crowd – if your roasting pot is large enough!

Serves 4
2 tbsp sunflower oil
1 chicken, weighing about 1.5 kg/3 lb
2 large oranges
2 small onions, quartered
500 g/1 lb/2 cups small whole carrots or thin carrots, cut into 5 cm/2 inch lengths
150ml/¼ pint/⅔ cup orange juice
2 tbsp brandy
2 tbsp sesame seeds
1 tbsp cornflour (cornstarch)
salt and pepper

1 Heat the oil in a large flameproof casserole and fry the chicken, turning occasionally until evenly browned.

2 Cut one orange in half and place half inside the cavity of the chicken. Place the chicken in a large, deep casserole. Arrange the onions and carrots around the chicken.

3 Season with salt and pepper and pour over the orange juice.

4 Cut the remaining oranges into thin wedges and tuck around the chicken, among the vegetables.

5 Cover and cook in a preheated oven, 180°C/350°F/Gas Mark 4, for about 1½ hours, or until there is no trace of pink in the chicken juices when pierced, and the vegetables are tender. Remove the lid and sprinkle with the brandy and sesame seeds, and return to the oven for 10 minutes.

6 To serve, lift the chicken onto a large platter and add the vegetables. Skim any excess fat from the juices.

Blend the cornflour with 1 tablespoon cold water, then stir into the juices and bring to the boil, stirring all the time. Adjust to taste, then serve the sauce with the chicken.

Poussin with Dried Fruits

Baby chickens are ideal for a one or two portion meal, and cook very easily and quickly for a special dinner. If you're cooking for one and it's not worth putting the oven on, a microwave makes cooking even quicker and more convenient. Use any mixture of dried fruits for a rich fruity flavour and colourful effect.

Serves 2

125 g/4 oz/³/₄ cup dried apples, peaches and prunes

120 ml/4 floz/¹/₂ cup boiling water

2 baby chickens

30 g/1 oz/¹/₃ cup walnut halves

1 tbsp honey

1 tsp ground allspice

1 tbsp walnut oil

salt and pepper

1 Place the fruits in a bowl, cover with the water and leave to stand for about 30 minutes.

2 Cut the chickens in half down the breastbone using a sharp knife, or leave whole.

3 Mix the fruit and any juices with the walnuts, honey and allspice and divide between two small roasting bags or squares of foil.

4 Brush the chickens with walnut oil and sprinkle with salt and pepper then place on top of the fruits.

5 Close the roasting bags or fold the foil over to enclose the chickens and bake on a baking sheet in a preheated oven, 190°C/375°F/Gas Mark 5, for 25–30 minutes or until the juices run clear. To cook in a microwave, use microwave roasting bags and cook on high/100% power for 6–7 minutes each, depending on size.

6 Serve hot with fresh vegetables and new potatoes.

COOK'S TIP

Alternative dried fruits that can be used in this recipe are cherries, mangoes or pawpaws.

Supreme of Chicken with Black Cherries

This recipe is rather time-consuming but it is well worth the effort.
Cherries and chicken make a good flavour combination.

Serves 6
6 large chicken supremes
6 black peppercorns, crushed
300 g/10 oz/2 cups pitted black cherries, or canned pitted cherries
12 shallots, sliced
4 slices rindless. streaky bacon, chopped
8 juniper berries
4 tbsp port
150 ml/$^1/_4$ pint/$^2/_3$ cup red wine
30 g/1 oz/2 tbsp butter
2 tbsp walnut oil
30 g/1 oz/$^1/_4$ cup flour
salt and pepper
black cherries and parsley, to garnish

1 Place the chicken in a large deep baking tin. Add the peppercorns, cherries or canned cherries, and their juice, if using, and the shallots.

2 Add the bacon, juniper berries, port and wine. Season well.

3 Place the chicken and marinade in the fridge for 48 hours.

4 Heat the butter and walnut oil in a large frying pan. Remove the chicken from the marinade and fry quickly in the pan for 4 minutes on each side.

5 Return the chicken to the marinade, reserving the butter, oil and juices in the pan.

6 Cover with foil and bake in a preheated oven, 180°C/350°F/Gas Mark 4, for 20 minutes. Transfer the chicken from the baking tin (pan) to a warm serving dish. Add the flour to the juices in the frying pan and cook for 4 minutes, add the marinade and bring to the boil then simmer for 10 minutes until the sauce is smooth.

7 Pour the sauce over the chicken supremes and garnish with black cherries and fresh parsley.

Roast Chicken in Wild Mushroom Sauce

This unusual chicken dish has the flavour of roast chicken but is finished off in a casserole with a wild mushroom sauce.

Serves 4
90 g/3 oz/^{1}/$_3$ cup butter, softened
1 garlic clove, crushed
1 large chicken
175 g/6 oz/2^1/$_4$ cups wild mushrooms
12 shallots
30 g/1 oz/2 tbsp plain flour
150 ml/^{1}/$_4$ pint/^{2}/$_3$ cup brandy
300 ml/^{1}/$_4$ pint/1^1/$_4$ cups double (heavy) cream
salt and pepper
1 tbsp chopped fresh parsley, to garnish

1 Place the butter, garlic, and salt and pepper in a bowl.

2 Rub the mixture inside and outside of the chicken and leave for 2 hours.

3 Place the chicken in a large roasting tin (pan) and roast in the centre of a preheated oven, 230°C/450°F/Gas Mark 8, for 1^1/$_2$ hours, basting every ten minutes.

4 Remove the chicken from the roasting tin (pan) and set aside to cool slightly.

5 Transfer the chicken juices to a saucepan and cook the mushrooms and shallots for 5 minutes. Sprinkle with the flour. Add the warm brandy and ignite.

6 Add the cream and cook for 3 minutes on a very low heat, stirring all the time.

7 Remove the bones and cut the chicken into small bite-sized pieces, then place the meat in a casserole dish. Cover with the mushroom sauce and bake in the oven, with the heat reduced to 160°C/325°F/Gas Mark 3, for a further 12 minutes. Garnish with the parsley and serve with wild rice or roast potatoes, and Brussel sprouts.

Honey & Mustard Baked Chicken

Chicken portions are brushed with a classic combination of honey and mustard then a crunchy coating of poppy seeds is added.

Serves 4–6
8 chicken portions
60 g/2 oz/4 tbsp butter, melted
4 tbsp mild mustard
4 tbsp clear honey
2 tbsp lemon juice
1 tsp paprika
3 tbsp poppy seeds
salt and pepper

1 Place the chicken pieces, skinless side down, on a large baking tray.

2 Place all the ingredients except the poppy seeds into a large bowl and blend together thoroughly.

3 Using a pastry brush, paint the mixture over the chicken portions.

4 Bake in the centre of a preheated oven, 200°C/400°F/Gas Mark 6, for 15 minutes.

5 Carefully turn over the chicken pieces, coating the top side of the chicken again.

6 Sprinkle the chicken with poppy seeds and return to the oven for a further 15 minutes.

7 Arrange the chicken on a serving dish, pour over the cooking juices and serve with a crisp salad.

Californian Chicken

It is better if you have time to bone the chicken completely,
or use chicken breast after removing all the fat and skin.

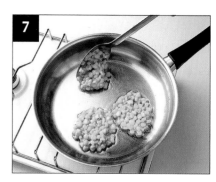

Serves 4–6

175 g/6 oz/1½ cups plain
(all-purpose) flour

1 tsp paprika

1 tsp freeze-dried
Italian seasoning

1 tsp freeze-dried tarragon

1 tsp rosemary, finely crushed

2 eggs, beaten

120 ml/4 fl oz/½ cup milk

1 chicken, weighing about
2 kg/4 lb, jointed

seasoned flour

150 ml/¼ pint/⅔ cup rapeseed oil

2 bananas, quartered

1 apple, cut into rings,

350 g/12 oz can sweetcorn
(corn-on-the-cob) & peppers, drained

oil for frying

salt and pepper

1 Mix together the flour, salt, spices
and herbs in a large bowl. Make a well
in the centre and add the eggs.

2 Blend and slowly add the milk,
whisking until very smooth.

3 Coat the chicken pieces with
seasoned flour and dip the chicken
pieces into the batter mix.

4 Heat the oil in a large frying pan.
Add the chicken and fry for about 3
minutes or until lightly browned all
over. Place the chicken pieces on a
non-stick baking tray.

5 Batter the bananas and apple rings
and fry for 2 minutes.

6 Finally toss the sweetcorn (corn-on-
the-cob) into the leftover batter.

7 Heat a little oil in a frying pan. Drop
in spoonfuls of the sweetcorn mixture
to make flat patty cakes. Cook for 4
minutes on each side. Keep warm
with the apple and banana fritters.

8 Bake the chicken in a preheated
oven, 200°C/400°F/Gas Mark 6, for

25 minutes until the chicken is tender
and golden brown.

9 Arrange the chicken, sweetcorn
fritters, and the apple and banana
fritters on a bed of fresh watercress.
Serve with a peppercorn or
horseradish sauce.

Springtime Roast Chicken

Baby chickens are simple to prepare, take about 30 minutes to roast and can be easily cut in half lengthways with a sharp knife. One baby chicken makes a substantial serving for each person. This combination of baby vegetables and baby chickens with a tangy low-fat sauce makes a healthy meal.

Serves 4
5 tbsp fresh brown breadcrumbs
200 g/7 oz/¹/₂ cup fromage frais or low-fat crème fraîche
5 tbsp chopped fresh parsley
5 tbsp chopped fresh chives
4 baby chickens
1 tbsp sunflower oil
675 g/1¹/₂ lb young spring vegetables such as carrots, courgettes (zucchini), sugar snap peas, corn (corn-on-the-cob) and turnips, cut into small chunks
120 ml/4 floz/¹/₂ cup boiling chicken stock
2 tsp cornflour (cornstarch)
150 ml/¹/₄ pint/²/₃ cup dry white wine
salt and pepper

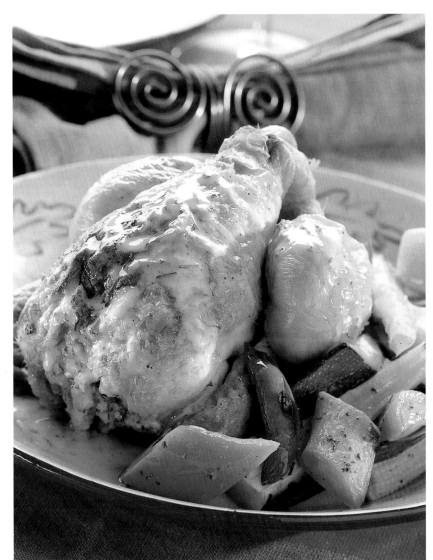

1 Mix together the breadcrumbs, one-third of the fromage frais and 2 tablespoons each of parsley and chives. Season well then spoon into the neck ends of the baby chickens. Place the chickens on a rack in a roasting tin (pan), brush with oil and season well.

2 Roast in a preheated oven, 220°C/425°F/Gas Mark 7, for 30–35 minutes or until the juices run clear, not pink, when the chickens are pierced with a skewer.

3 Place the vegetables in a shallow ovenproof dish in one layer and add half the remaining herbs with the stock. Cover and bake for 25–30 minutes until tender. Lift the chickens onto a serving plate and skim any fat from the juices in the tin. Add the vegetable juices.

4 Blend the cornflour (cornstarch) with the wine and whisk into the sauce with the remaining fromage frais. Whisk until boiling, then add the remaining herbs. Season to taste. Spoon the sauce over the chickens and serve with the vegetables.

Mediterranean Style Sunday Roast

A roast that is full of Mediterranean flavour. A mixture of feta cheese, rosemary
and sun-dried tomatoes is stuffed under the chicken skin,
then roasted with garlic, new potatoes and vegetables.

Serves 6
2.5 kg/5¹/₂ lb chicken
sprigs of fresh rosemary
175 g/6 oz/³/₄ cup feta cheese, coarsely grated
2 tbsp sun-dried tomato paste
60 g/2 oz/4 tbsp butter, softened
1 bulb garlic
1 kg/2 lb new potatoes, halved if large
1 each red, green and yellow (bell) pepper, cut into chunks
3 courgettes (zucchini), sliced thinly
2 tbsp olive oil
2 tbsp plain (all-purpose) flour
600 ml/1pint/2¹/₂ cups chicken stock
salt and pepper

1 Rinse the chicken inside and out with cold water and drain well. Carefully cut between the skin and the top of the breast meat using a small pointed knife. Slide a finger into the slit and carefully enlarge it to form a pocket. Continue until the skin is completely lifted away from both breasts and the top of the legs.

2 Chop the leaves from 3 rosemary stems. Mix with the feta, sun-dried tomato paste, butter and pepper then spoon under the skin. Put the chicken in a large roasting tin (pan), cover with foil and cook in a preheated oven, 190°C/375°F/Gas Mark 5, for 20 minutes per 500g/1lb plus 20 minutes.

3 Break the garlic bulb into cloves but do not peel. Add the vegetables to the chicken after 40 minutes.

4 Drizzle with oil, tuck in a few stems of rosemary and season well. Cook for the remaining time, removing the foil for the last 40 minutes to brown the chicken.

5 Transfer the chicken to a serving platter. Place some of the vegetables around the chicken and transfer the remainder to a warmed serving dish. Pour the fat out of the roasting tin and stir the flour into the remaining pan juices. Cook for 2 minutes then gradually stir in the stock. Bring to the boil, stirring until thickened and smooth. Strain into a sauce boat and garnish the chicken with rosemary.

Chicken with Marmalade Stuffing

Marmalade lovers will enjoy this festive recipe. You can use any favourite marmalade, such as lemon or grapefruit.

Serves 6
1 chicken, weighing about 2.25 kg/5 lb
bay leaves
2 tbsp marmalade

STUFFING
1 stick (stalk) celery, chopped finely
1 small onion, chopped finely
1 tbsp sunflower oil
125 g/4 oz/2 cups fresh wholemeal (whole wheat) breadcrumbs
4 tbsp marmalade
2 tbsp chopped fresh parsley
1 egg, beaten
salt and pepper

SAUCE
2 tsp cornflour (cornstarch)
2 tbsp orange juice
3 tbsp marmalade
150 ml/$^1/_4$ pint/$^2/_3$ cup chicken stock
1 medium orange
2 tbsp brandy
orange slices, bay leaves or celery leaves, to garnish

1 Lift the neck flap of the chicken and remove the wishbone using a small, sharp knife.

2 Place a sprig of bay leaves inside the body cavity of the bird.

3 To make the stuffing, sauté the celery and onion in the oil to soften. Add the breadcrumbs, 3 tablespoons of marmalade, parsley and egg. Season. Stuff the neck cavity of the chicken with the mixture. Any extra stuffing may be cooked separately.

4 Place the chicken in a roasting tin (pan) and brush lightly with oil. Roast in a preheated oven, 190°C/375°F/Gas Mark 5 for 20 minutes per 500 g/1 lb plus 20 minutes or until the juices run clear. Remove from the oven and glaze with the remaining marmalade.

5 Meanwhile, to make the sauce, blend the cornflour in a pan with the orange juice, then add the marmalade and stock. Heat gently, stirring, until thickened and smooth. Remove from the heat. Cut the segments from the orange, discarding all white pith and membrane. Just before serving, add to the sauce with the brandy and bring to the boil before serving with the chicken. Garnish with orange slices and bay leaves or celery leaves.

Pollo Catalan

The Catalan region of Spain is famous for its wonderful combinations of meat with fruit. Nuts and spices are often added too. In this recipe, peaches lend a touch of sweetness and pine nuts, cinnamon and sherry add an unusual twist. Canned peach halves in natural juice make an easy storecupboard alternative.

Serves 6
60 g/2 oz/1 cup fresh brown breadcrumbs
60 g/2 oz/$^1/_2$ cup pine nuts
1 small egg, beaten
4 tbsp chopped fresh thyme or 1 tbsp dried thyme
4 fresh peaches or 8 canned peach halves
1 chicken, weighing about 2 5 kg/5$^1/_2$ lb
1 tsp ground cinnamon
200 ml/7 fl oz/$^3/_4$ cup Amontillado sherry
4 tbsp double (heavy) cream
salt and pepper

1 Combine the breadcrumbs with 30 g/1 oz/¼ cup pine nuts, the egg and the thyme.

2 Halve and stone the fresh peaches, and remove the skin if necessary. Dice one peach into small pieces and stir into the breadcrumb mixture. Season well with salt and pepper. Spoon the stuffing into the neck cavity of the chicken, securing the skin firmly over it.

3 Place the chicken in a roasting tin (pan) and sprinkle the cinnamon over the skin.

4 Cover loosely with foil and roast in a preheated oven, 190°C/375°F/Gas Mark 5, for 1 hour, basting occasionally.

5 Remove the foil and spoon the sherry over the chicken. Cook for a

further 30 minutes, basting with the sherry juices, until the juices run clear when the chicken is pierced with a skewer. Sprinkle the remaining pine nuts over the remaining peach halves and place in an ovenproof dish in the oven for the final 10 minutes of cooking time.

6 Lift the chicken onto a serving plate and arrange the peaches around it. Skim any fat from the juices, stir in the cream and heat gently. Serve with the chicken.

Whisky Roast Chicken

An unusual change from a plain roast, with a distinctly warming Scottish flavour and a delicious oatmeal stuffing.

Serves 6
1 chicken, weighing 2 kg/4 lb
1 tbsp heather honey
2 tbsp Scotch whisky
2 tbsp plain (all-purpose) flour
300 ml/¹/₂ pint/1¹/₄ cups chicken stock

STUFFING
1 medium onion, finely chopped
1 stick (stalk) celery, sliced thinly
1 tbsp butter or sunflower oil
1 tsp dried thyme
4 tbsp porridge oats
4 tbsp chicken stock
salt and pepper

1 To make the stuffing, fry the onion and celery in the butter or oil, stirring over a moderate heat until softened and lightly browned.

2 Remove from the heat and stir in the thyme, oats, stock, salt and pepper.

3 Stuff the neck end of the chicken with the mixture and tuck the neck flap under. Place in a roasting tin, (pan) brush lightly with oil, and roast in a preheated oven, 190°C/375°F/Gas Mark 5, for about 1 hour.

4 Mix the honey with 1 tablespoon whisky and brush the mixture over the chicken. Return to the oven for a further 20 minutes, or until the chicken is golden brown and the juices run clear when pierced through the thickest part with a skewer.

5 Lift the chicken onto a serving plate. Skim the fat from the juices then stir in the flour. Stir over a moderate heat until the mixture bubbles, then gradually add the stock and remaining whisky.

6 Bring to the boil, stirring, then simmer for 1 minute and serve the chicken with the sauce, green vegetable and sauté potatoes.

Gardener's Chicken

Any combination of small, young vegetables can be roasted with the chicken, such as courgettes (zucchini), leeks and onions.

Serves 4
250 g/8 oz/4 cups parsnips, peeled and chopped
125 g/4 oz/^{3}/$_4$ cup carrots, peeled and chopped
30 g/1 oz/^{1}/$_2$ cup fresh breadcrumbs
^{1}/$_4$ tsp grated nutmeg
1 tbsp chopped fresh parsley
1.5 kg/3 lb chicken
bunch parsley
^{1}/$_2$ onion
30 g/1 oz/2 tbsp butter, softened
4 tbsp olive oil
500 g/1lb new potatoes, scrubbed
500 g/1lb baby carrots washed and trimmed
salt and pepper

1 To make the stuffing, put the parsnips and carrots into a pan, half cover with water and bring to the boil. Cover the pan and simmer until tender. Drain well then purée in a blender or food processor. Transfer the purée to a bowl and leave to cool.

2 Mix in the breadcrumbs, nutmeg and parsley and season with salt and pepper.

3 Put the stuffing into the neck end of the chicken and push a little under the skin over the breast meat. Secure the flap of skin with a small metal skewer or cocktail stick.

4 Place the bunch of parsley and onion inside the cavity of the chicken, then place the chicken in a large roasting tin (pan).

5 Spread the butter over the skin and season with salt and pepper, cover with foil and place the chicken in a preheated oven, 190°C/375°F/Gas Mark 5, for 30 minutes.

6 Meanwhile, heat the oil in a frying pan, and lightly brown the potatoes.

7 Transfer the potatoes to the roasting tin and add the baby carrots. Baste the chicken and continue to cook for a further hour, basting the chicken and vegetable after 30 minutes.Remove the foil for the last 20 minutes to allow the skin to crisp.

Festive Apple Chicken

The richly flavoured stuffing in this recipe is cooked
under the breast skin of the chicken, so not only is all the flavour sealed in,
but the chicken stays really moist and succulent during cooking.

Serves 6
1 chicken, weighing 2 kg/ 4 lb
2 dessert apples
15 g/¹/₂ oz/1 tbsp butter
1 tbsp redcurrant jelly
parsley, to garnish

STUFFING
15 g/¹/₂ oz/1 tbsp butter
1 small onion, chopped finely
60 g/2 oz mushrooms, chopped finely
60 g/2 oz smoked ham, chopped finely
30 g/1 oz/¹/₂ cup fresh breadcrumbs
1 tbsp chopped fresh parsley
1 crisp eating apple
1 tbsp lemon juice
oil, to brush
salt and pepper

1 To make the stuffing, melt the butter and fry the onion gently, stirring until softened but not browned. Stir in the mushrooms and cook over a moderate heat for 2–3 minutes. Remove from the heat and stir in the ham, breadcrumbs and the chopped parsley.

2 Core the apple, leaving the skin on, and grate coarsely. Add the stuffing mixture to the apple with the lemon juice. Season to taste.

3 Loosen the breast skin of the chicken and carefully spoon the stuffing mixture under it, smoothing evenly with your hands.

4 Place the chicken in a roasting tin (pan) and brush lightly with oil.

5 Roast the chicken in a preheated oven, 190°C/375°F/Gas Mark 5, for 25 minutes per 500 g/1 lb plus 25 minutes, or until there is no trace of pink in the juices when the chicken is pierced through the thickest part with a skewer. If the breast starts to brown too much, cover the chicken with foil.

6 Core and slice the remaining apples and sauté in the butter until golden. Stir in the redcurrant jelly and warm through until melted. Serve the chicken garnished with the apple slices and parsley.

Chicken with Creamy Courgette (Zucchini) & Lime Stuffing

A cheesy stuffing is tucked under the breast skin of the chicken
to give added flavour and moistness to the meat.

Serves 6

1 chicken, weighing 2.25 kg/5 lb

oil for brushing

250 g/8 oz/1¹/₃ cups courgette (zucchini)

30 g/1 oz/2 tbsp butter

juice of 1 lime

lime slices and shreds of lime rind, to garnish

STUFFING

90 g/3 oz/¹/₂ cup courgette (zucchini)

90 g/3 oz/³/₄ cup medium-fat soft cheese

finely grated rind of1 lime

2 tbsp fresh breadcrumbs

salt and pepper

or sharp knife. Sauté in the butter and lime juice until just tender, then serve with the chicken. Garnish with lime slices and shreds of lime rind.

COOK'S TIP

For quicker cooking, finely grate the courgettes (zucchini) rather than cutting them into strips.

1 To make the stuffing, trim and coarsely grate the courgette (zucchini) and mix with the cheese, lime rind, breadcrumbs, salt and pepper.

2 Carefully ease the skin away from the breast of the chicken with the fingertips, taking care not to split it.

3 Push the stuffing under the skin, to cover the breast evenly.

4 Place in a baking tin (pan), brush with oil and roast in a preheated oven, 190°C/ 375°F/Gas Mark 5, for 20 minutes per 500 g/1 lb plus 20 minutes, or until the chicken juices run clear when pierced with a skewer.

5 Meanwhile, trim the remaining courgettes (zucchini) and cut into long, thin strips with a potato peeler

Cheddar Baked Chicken

Cheese and mustard, and a simple, crispy coating, make a delicious combination for this healthy dish.

Serves 4
1 tbsp milk
2 tbsp prepared English mustard
60 g/2oz/1 cup grated mature Cheddar cheese
3 tbsp plain (all-purpose) flour
2 tbsp chopped fresh chives
4 skinless, boneless chicken breasts

1 Mix together the milk and mustard in a bowl. Mix the cheese with the flour and chives on a plate.

2 Dip the chicken into the milk and mustard mixture, brushing with a pastry brush to coat evenly.

3 Dip the chicken breasts into the cheese mixture, pressing to coat them evenly all over.

4 Place on a baking sheet and spoon any spare cheese coating on top.

5 Bake the chicken in a preheated oven, 200°C/400°F/Gas Mark 6, for 30–35 minutes, or until golden brown and the juices run clear, not pink, when pierced with a skewer. Serve the chicken hot, with jacket potatoes and fresh vegetables, or serve cold, with a crisp salad.

Feta Chicken with Mountain Herbs

Chicken goes well with most savoury herbs, especially during the summer, when fresh herbs are at their best. This combination makes a good partner for tangy feta cheese and sun-ripened tomatoes.

Serves 4

8 skinless, boneless chicken thighs

2 tbsp each chopped fresh thyme, rosemary and oregano

125 g/4 oz/^{1}/$_2$ cup feta cheese

salt and pepper

1 tbsp milk

2 tbsp plain (all-purpose) flour

salt and pepper

thyme, rosemary and oregano, to garnish

TOMATO SAUCE

1 medium onion, roughly chopped

1 garlic clove, crushed

1 tbsp olive oil

4 medium plum tomatoes, quartered

sprig each of thyme, rosemary and oregano

1 Spread out the chicken thighs on a board, smooth side downwards.

2 Divide the herbs among the chicken thighs, then cut the cheese into eight sticks. Place one stick of cheese in the centre of each chicken thigh. Season well, then roll up to enclose the cheese.

3 Place the rolls in an ovenproof dish, brush with milk and dust with flour to coat evenly.

4 Bake in a preheated oven, 190°C/375°F/Gas Mark 5, for 25–30 minutes, or until golden brown. There should be no pink in the juices when the chicken is pierced with a skewer.

5 To make the sauce, cook the onion and garlic in the olive oil, stirring, until softened and beginning to brown.

6 Add the tomatoes, reduce the heat, cover tightly and simmer gently for 15–20 minutes or until soft.

7 Add the herbs, then transfer to a food processor and blend to a purée. Press through a sieve to make a smooth, rich sauce. Season to taste and serve the sauce with the chicken, garnished with herbs.

Honeyed Citrus Chicken

This fat-free recipe is great for summer entertaining served simply with a green salad and new potatoes. If you cut the chicken in half and press it flat, you can roast it in under an hour.

Serves 4
2 kg/4 lb chicken
salt and pepper
tarragon sprigs, to garnish

MARINADE

300 ml/½ pint/1¼ cups orange juice
3 tbsp cider vinegar
3 tbsp clear honey
2 tbsp chopped fresh tarragon
2 oranges, cut into wedges

SAUCE

handful of tarragon sprigs
200 g/7 oz/1 cup fat-free fromage frais
2 tbsp orange juice
1 tsp clear honey
60 g/2 oz/½ cup stuffed olives, chopped

1 Put the chicken on a chopping board with the breast downwards. Cut through the bottom part of the carcass using poultry shears or heavy kitchen scissors, making sure not to cut right through to the breast bone below.

2 Rinse the chicken with cold water, drain and place on a board with the skin side uppermost. Press the chicken flat, then cut off the leg ends.

3 Thread two long wooden skewers through the bird to keep it flat and season the skin with salt and pepper.

4 Put all the marinade ingredients, except the orange wedges, in a shallow, non-metallic dish. Mix, then add the chicken. Cover and chill for 4 hours. Turn the chicken several times.

5 To make the sauce, chop the tarragon, and mix with the sauce ingredients. Season and spoon into a serving dish. Cover and chill.

6 Transfer the chicken and marinade to a roasting tin (pan), open out the chicken and place skin-side downwards. Tuck the orange wedges around the chicken and roast in a preheated oven, 200°C/400°F/Gas Mark 6, for 25 minutes.

7 Turn the chicken over and roast for another 20–30 minutes. Baste until the chicken is browned and the juices run clear when the thickest part of the leg is pierced with a skewer. Garnish with tarragon, carve into thin slices and serve with the sauce.

Chicken with Baby Onions & Green Peas

Pork fat adds a tasty flavour to this dish. If you can't find fresh garden peas, frozen peas are a good substitute.

Serves 4
250 g/8 oz/1 cup pork fat, cut into small cubes
60 g/2 oz/4 tbsp butter
16 small onions or shallots
1 kg/2 lb boneless chicken pieces
30 g/1 oz/¼ cup plain (all-purpose) flour
600 ml/1 pint/2½ cups chicken stock
500 g/1 lb/4 cups fresh peas
bouquet garni
salt and pepper

1 Place the pork fat cubes in a pan of boiling salted water and simmer for three minutes then drain and dry.

2 Melt the butter in a large frying pan, add the pork and onions, fry gently for 3 minutes until lightly browned.

3 Remove the pork and onions from the pan, add the chicken pieces and brown them all over. Remove them from the pan and transfer the chicken to a baking tray.

4 Add the flour to the pan and cook, stirring until it begins to brown, then slowly blend in the chicken stock.

5 Cook the chicken, with the sauce and bouquet garni, in a preheated oven, 200°C/400°F/Gas Mark 6, for 35 minutes.

6 Remove the bouquet garni about 10 minutes before the end of cooking time and add the onions, pork and peas. Stir to mix.

7 When cooked, place the chicken pieces onto a large platter, surrounded with the pork, peas, onions

COOK'S TIP

If you want to cut down on fat, use lean bacon, cut into small cubes, rather than pork fat.

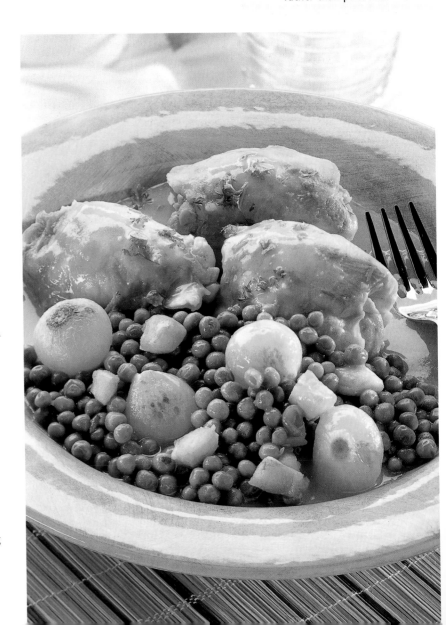

Traditional Roast Chicken

Roast chicken is an all-time classic which pleases everyone.
Serve it with bread sauce for a delicious meal.

Serves 4–6
1 roasting chicken, weighing about 2 kg/4 lb,
60 g/2 oz/¼ cup butter
1 kg/2 lb potatoes, cut into even pieces
4 slices streaky bacon
8 chipolata sausages

STUFFING
60 g/2 oz/1 cup soft white breadcrumbs
125 g/4 oz/²/₃ cup minced pork sausagemeat
1 tbsp each chopped mixed fresh herbs & sage

BREAD SAUCE
300 ml/½ pint/1¼ cups milk
90g/3 oz crustless white bread
1 onion, pierced with 10 cloves
30 g/1 oz/2 tbsp butter
pinch ground allspice
1 tbsp double (heavy) cream
1 tbsp plain (all-purpose) flour
150 ml/¼ pint/²/₃ cup chicken stock
2–3 tbsp sherry

1 To make the stuffing, mix the breadcrumbs, sausagemeat, mixed herbs and sage. Spoon the stuffing through the neck end of the bird, using the loose skin to make a full pocket of stuffing.

2 Fasten the flap of skin underneath , with string. Put any remaining stuffing in the cavity at the other end. Transfer to a roasting tin (pan), and rub with butter. Cover with parchment and bake in a preheated oven, 200°C/400°F/Gas Mark 6, for 20 minutes. Reduce the heat to 180°C/350°F/Gas Mark 4 for 1 hour and 20 minutes. Remove the parchment and baste the chicken.

3 Meanwhile, parboil the potatoes, then drain. Add to the chicken, and coat in the fat. Roast for 1 hour.

4 Cut the bacon in half, stretch with a knife, wrap around the sausages, and roast with the chicken for 30 minutes.

5 To make the bread sauce, put all the ingredients in a saucepan together and simmer for 30 minutes. Remove the onion before serving hot.

6 Remove the parchment 15 minutes before the chicken has cooked, and crisp the skin. Leave the chicken to rest for 20 minutes, in a warm place, while you make the gravy. Serve with the roast potatoes and the chipolatas, and accompanied by the bread sauce.

Golden Chicken with Mango & Cranberries

This recipe, which uses a partly-boned chicken is easy to slice and serve. If you prefer, stuff in the traditional way at the neck end, and cook any remaining stuffing separately.

Serves 6
1 chicken, weighing about 2.25 kg/5 lb
6 slices smoked bacon

STUFFING
1 ripe mango, diced
50g/2oz/$\frac{1}{4}$ cup fresh or frozen cranberries
125 g/4 oz/2 cups breadcrumbs
$\frac{1}{2}$ tsp ground mace
1 egg, beaten
salt and pepper

GLAZE
$\frac{1}{2}$ tsp ground turmeric
2 tsp honey
2 tsp sunflower oil
mango slices and cranberries, to garnish

1 To part-bone the chicken, dislocate the legs and place the chicken breast-side downwards.

2 With a sharp knife, cut a straight line through the skin along the ridge of the back.

3 Carefully scrape the meat down from the bone on both sides.

4 When you reach the point where the legs and wings join the body, cut through the joints. Work around the ribcage until the carcass can be lifted away. Make six bacon rolls. Mix the mango with the cranberries, breadcrumbs and mace, then bind with egg. Season with salt and pepper.

5 Place the chicken, skin-side down, and spoon over half the stuffing.

Arrange the bacon rolls down the centre then top with the remaining stuffing. Fold the skin over and tie with string. Turn the chicken over, truss the legs and tuck the wings underneath. Place in a roasting tin. To make the glaze, mix the turmeric, honey and oil and brush over the skin.

6 Roast in a preheated oven, 190°C/375°F/Gas Mark 5, for 1½–2 hours or until the juices run clear, not pink, when the chicken is pierced. Cover loosely with foil once the chicken is browned, to prevent overbrowning. Serve the chicken hot with seasonal vegetables.

Boned Chicken with Parmesan

It's really very easy to bone a whole chicken, but if you prefer,
you can ask a friendly butcher to do this for you.

Serves 6
1 chicken, weighing about 2.25 kg/5 lb
8 slices Mortadella or salami
125 g/4 oz/2 cups fresh white or brown breadcrumbs
125 g/4 oz/1 cup freshly grated Parmesan cheese
2 garlic cloves, crushed
6 tbsp chopped fresh basil or parsley
1 egg, beaten
pepper

1 Bone the chicken, keeping the skin intact. Dislocate each leg by breaking it at the thigh joint. Cut down each side of the backbone, taking care not to pierce the breast skin.

2 Pull the backbone clear of the flesh and discard. Remove the ribs, severing any attached flesh with a sharp knife.

3 Scrape away all the flesh from each leg and cut away the bone at the joint with a knife or shears.

4 Use the bones for stock. Lay out the boned chicken on a board, skin side down. Arrange the Mortadella slices over the chicken, overlapping slightly.

5 Combine the breadcrumbs, Parmesan, garlic and basil, season well with pepper and stir in the beaten egg to bind. Pile the mixture down the middle of the boned chicken, roll the meat around it and tie securely with fine cotton string.

6 Place in a roasting dish and brush lightly with olive oil. Roast in a preheated oven, 200°C/400°F/Gas Mark 6, for 1½ hours or until the juices run clear when pierced.

7 Serve hot or cold, in slices, with fresh spring vegetables.

Casseroles

Long, slow cooking means meltingly
succulent meat with a good, rich flavour.
Because chicken itself does not have a
strong flavour, it marries happily with
almost any other ingredient and the recipes
in this section exploit that quality. They are
drawn from many cuisines from around the
world, and there are dishes from Italy,
France, Hungary, Asia, the Caribbean, and

from the USA.
French classics
include Coq au Vin
Blanc, Garlic
Chicken Cassoulet,
Bourguignonne of
Chicken, and

Chicken with 40 Garlic Cloves, a recipe that
is not as daunting as it sounds. After
cooking, the garlic becomes surprisingly
mild and sweet. Chicken also makes a
good partner for olives, beans and rice, and
pilaus and jambalayas are just some of the
dishes on offer. Spicy Cajun recipes include
Chicken Etouffé and Grillades with Grits.

Chicken Cacciatore

This is a popular Italian classic in which browned chicken quarters
are cooked in a richly flavoured sauce of tomatoes and peppers.

Serves 4

1 roasting chicken, weighing
1.5 kg/3 lb, cut into
6 or 8 serving pieces

120 g/4 oz/1 cup plain
(all-purpose) flour

3 tbsp olive oil

150 ml/$^{1}/_{4}$ pt/$^{2}/_{3}$ cup dry white wine

1 green (bell) pepper,
sliced

1 red (bell) pepper,
sliced

1 carrot, chopped finely

1 celery stick (stalk), chopped finely

1 garlic clove, crushed

200 g/7 oz can of chopped
tomatoes

salt and pepper

1 Rinse and pat dry the chicken pieces.

2 Lightly dust them with seasoned
flour and brown them over a medium
heat in the olive oil. When browned
all over, set the pieces aside.

3 Drain off all but 2 tablespoons of
the fat in the pan, add the wine and
stir for a few minutes. Add the
peppers, carrot, celery and garlic,
season well and simmer together for
about 15 minutes.

4 Add the chopped tomatoes and the
chicken pieces to the pan. Cover and
simmer for 30 minutes, stirring often,
until the chicken is cooked.

5 Check the seasoning before serving
piping hot.

Chicken with 40 Garlic Cloves

In France, the chicken is served accompanied by slices of bread. Each diner spreads the bread with the softened and sweetened garlic.

Serves 4
1 roasting chicken, weighing about 1.5 kg/ 3 lb
15 g/$^{1}/_{2}$ oz/$^{1}/_{2}$ cup fresh thyme
15 g/$^{1}/_{2}$ oz/$^{1}/_{2}$ cup fresh rosemary
15 g/$^{1}/_{2}$ oz/$^{1}/_{2}$ cup fresh sage
15 g/$^{1}/_{2}$ oz/$^{1}/_{2}$ cup fresh parsley
2 small celery sticks (stalks)
40 fresh garlic cloves, unpeeled
4 tbsp olive oil
salt and pepper

1 Wash and pat dry the chicken and rub salt into the skin.

2 Stuff the cavity with half of the fresh herbs, celery, and 10 of the garlic cloves.

3 Place the chicken in a roasting tin (pan) or earthenware dish, arrange the rest of the herbs, celery and garlic around the chicken, and smear oil all over the skin.

4 Roast in a preheated oven, 200°C/400°F/Gas Mark 6, for 1½ hours, basting frequently.

5 Transfer the cooked chicken to a warmed serving platter, and surround with the cloves of garlic. Skim most of the fat from the cooking juices, bring to the boil in the pan, and reduce slightly. Strain into a warmed sauce boat to serve.

Chicken & Black Beans (Peas)

In India and Pakistan, pulses are a valuable source of nourishment in mountainous areas in the winter, when meat is scarce. You could use any variety of pulses in this recipe, but adjust the cooking times accordingly.

Serves 4

250 g/8 oz/1 generous cup dried black-eye beans (peas), soaked overnight and drained

1 tsp salt

2 onions, chopped

2 garlic cloves, crushed

1 tsp ground turmeric

1 tsp ground cumin

1.25 kg/2½ lb chicken, jointed into 8 pieces

1 green (bell) pepper, chopped

2 tbsp oil

2.5 cm/1 inch piece fresh ginger root, grated

2 tsp coriander seeds

½ tsp fennel seeds

2 tsp garam masala

1 tbsp chopped fresh coriander (cilantro), to garnish

1 Put the drained beans into a wok or large frying pan (skillet) with the salt, onions, garlic, turmeric and cumin. Cover with water, bring to the boil and cook for 15 minutes.

2 Add the chicken and (bell) pepper to the pan and bring to the boil. Lower the heat and simmer for 30 minutes until the juices run clear with no trace of pink when the thickest parts of the chicken pieces are pierced with a sharp knife.

3 Heat the oil in a clean pan and fry the ginger, coriander seeds and fennel seeds for 30 seconds.

4 Add this mixture to the chicken with the garam masala. Simmer for a further 5 minutes and serve garnished with fresh coriander (cilantro).

Chicken & Chilli Bean Pot

This Mexican aromatic chicken dish has a spicy kick. Chicken thighs are not only more economical than breasts, they have much more flavour when cooked in this way.

Serves 4
2 tbsp plain (all-purpose) flour
1 tsp chilli powder
8 chicken thighs or 4 chicken legs
3 tbsp olive or vegetable oil
2 garlic cloves, crushed
1 large onion, chopped
1 green or red (bell) pepper, chopped
300 ml/$\frac{1}{2}$ pint/1$\frac{1}{4}$ cups chicken stock
2 medium tomatoes, chopped
425 g/14 oz can of red kidney beans, rinsed and drained
2 tbsp tomato purée (paste)
salt and pepper

1 Mix together the flour, chilli powder, and salt and pepper in a shallow dish. Rinse the chicken, but do not dry. Dip the chicken into the seasoned flour, coating it on all sides.

2 Heat the oil in a large, deep frying pan (skillet) or saucepan and add the chicken. Cook over a high heat for 3–4 minutes, turning the pieces to brown them all over. Remove with a perforated spoon and drain on absorbent paper towels.

3 Add the garlic, onion and (bell) pepper to the pan and fry gently for 2–3 minutes until softened.

4 Add the stock, tomatoes, kidney beans and tomato purée (paste), stirring well. Bring to the boil.

5 Return the chicken to the pan. Reduce the heat and simmer, covered, for about 30 minutes, until the chicken is tender. Season with salt and pepper to taste. Transfer to a warm serving dish and serve at once.

COOK'S TIP

Serve this spicy dish with boiled rice or warmed tortillas, with a side dish of soured cream or natural yogurt.

Chicken with Green Olives

Olives are a popular flavouring for poultry and game in Apulia in Italy, where this recipe originates. In Italy every bit of the bird is used in some way, most often for soups and stock.

Serves 4
4 chicken breasts, part boned
2 tbsp olive oil
30 g/1 oz/2 tbsp butter
1 large onion, chopped finely
2 garlic cloves, crushed
2 red, yellow or green (bell) peppers, cut into large pieces
250 g/8 oz/3 cups large closed-cup mushrooms, sliced or quartered
2 small tomatoes, peeled and halved
150 ml/¼ pint/⅔ cup dry white wine
125 g/4 oz/1 cup green olives, pitted
4–6 tbsp double (heavy) cream
salt and pepper
chopped flat-leafed parsley, to garnish
pasta or tiny new potatoes, to serve

1 Season the chicken with salt and pepper. Heat the oil and butter in a frying pan (skillet), add the chicken and fry until browned all over. Remove from the pan and keep warm.

2 Add the onion and garlic to the pan and fry gently until beginning to soften. Add the (bell) peppers and the mushrooms and continue to cook for a few minutes longer.

3 Add the tomatoes and plenty of seasoning to the pan, and then transfer the vegetable mixture to an ovenproof casserole. Place the chicken on the bed of vegetables.

4 Add the wine to the pan and bring to the boil. Pour the wine over the chicken and cover the casserole. Cook in a preheated oven, 180°C/350°F/Gas Mark 4, for 50 minutes.

5 Add the olives to the chicken, mix lightly then pour on the cream. Re-cover the casserole and return to the oven for 10–20 minutes or until the chicken is very tender.

6 Adjust the seasoning and serve the pieces of chicken, surrounded by the vegetables and sauce, with pasta or tiny new potatoes. Sprinkle with parsley to garnish.

Roman Chicken

This Roman dish is equally good cold and could be taken
on a picnic – serve with bread to mop up the juices.

Serves 4
4 tbsp olive oil
6 chicken pieces
4 large mixed red, green and yellow (bell) peppers
1 large red onion, sliced
2 garlic cloves, crushed with 1 tsp salt
125 g/4 oz/^{2}/$_3$ cup pitted green olives
Tomato Sauce (page 138)
300 ml/^{1}/$_2$ pint/1^1/$_4$ cups hot chicken stock
2 sprigs fresh marjoram
salt and pepper

1 Heat half the oil in a flameproof casserole and brown the chicken pieces on all sides. Remove the chicken pieces and set aside.

2 Remove the seeds and the cores from the (bell) pepper and cut them into strips.

3 Add the remaining oil to the casserole. Fry the onion gently for 5–7 minutes until just softened, then add the garlic and fry for another minute. Stir in the (bell) peppers, olives and tomato sauce and bring to the boil.

4 Return the chicken to the casserole with the stock and the marjoram. Cover the casserole and simmer for about 45 minutes until the chicken is tender. Season to taste with salt and pepper and serve with crusty bread.

Coq au Vin Blanc

Small pieces of chicken are gently simmered with wine, herbs, bacon, mushrooms and onions to produce a dish reminiscent of an authentic French meal.

Serves 2
2 chicken leg quarters
4 thick lean back bacon slices, derinded
2 tbsp oil
8 button onions or 1 large onion, sliced
1 garlic clove, crushed
150 ml/¼ pint/⅔ cup dry white wine
300 ml/½ pint/1¼ cups chicken stock
1 bay leaf
large pinch of dried oregano
1 tbsp cornflour (cornstarch)
60 g/2 oz/¾ cup tiny button mushrooms, trimmed
salt and pepper
chopped fresh parsley, to garnish
boiled rice or creamed potatoes, to serve

1 Cut each chicken leg into two pieces and season well with salt and pepper. Cut the bacon into 1 cm/½ inch strips.

2 Heat the oil in a saucepan. Fry the chicken until golden brown and remove from the pan. Add the bacon, onions and garlic, and fry until browned. Drain the fat from the pan.

3 Add the wine, stock, bay leaf, oregano, and salt and pepper to the saucepan. Return the chicken to the pan and bring to the boil.

4 Cover the saucepan tightly and simmer very gently for about 40–50 minutes, or until the chicken is tender and cooked through and the juices run clear when pierced with a skewer.

5 Blend the cornflour (cornstarch) with a little cold water and add to the saucepan with the mushrooms. Bring back to the boil and simmer for a further 5 minutes.

6 Adjust the seasoning and discard the bay leaf. Serve sprinkled liberally with chopped parsley, and with boiled rice or creamed potatoes.

Country Chicken Casserole

Most ceramic casserole dishes can be used with care on the hob, but a diffuser can be placed between the heat and the dish – it is usually a double layer of perforated metal holding the dish off the heat. However, you can simply sauté the chicken then transfer it to an ovenproof dish.

Serves 4
1 free-range chicken, 1.5 kg/ 3 lb, cut into pieces
flour for dusting
30 g/1 oz/¼ cup butter
1 tsp olive oil
10 pickling onions
3 cloves garlic, unpeeled
1 carrot, diced
1 celery stick (stalk), diced
1 bay leaf
125 g/4 oz/⅔ cup smoked streaky bacon, diced
600 ml/1 pint/2½ cups stock, or to cover
750 g/1½ lb waxy potatoes, sliced
salt and pepper

1 Rinse and pat dry the chicken pieces. Dust with flour. Melt the butter with the oil over medium-high heat and brown the chicken pieces well all over. Set aside.

2 Add the onions, garlic, carrot, celery, bay leaf and bacon to the pan. Cook over a medium heat for 10 minutes, and season well. Return the chicken to the pan and pour on the stock. Check the seasoning.

3 Arrange the sliced potatoes over the top of the casserole. Cover and simmer for 1 hour.

4 Serve piping hot with a selection of green vegetables.

Chicken with Rice & Peas

This dish, which is also known as chicken pelau, is a national favourite
in Trinidad and Tobago. The secret of a good pelau is that it must be brown in colour,
which is achieved by caramelizing the chicken first.

Serves 6
1 onion, chopped
2 garlic cloves
1 tbsp chopped fresh chives
1 tbsp chopped fresh thyme
2 celery sticks (stalks) with leaves, chopped
350 ml/12 fl oz/1½ cups water
½ fresh coconut, chopped
liquid from 1 fresh coconut
500 g/16 oz can pigeon peas, drained
1 fresh red chilli, deseeded and cut into strips
2 tbsp groundnut oil
2 tbsp caster (superfine) sugar
1.5 kg/3 lb chicken pieces
250 g/8 oz/generous 1 cup long-grain rice, rinsed and drained
salt and pepper
celery leaves, to garnish

1 Put the onion, garlic, chives, thyme,
celery and 4 tablespoons of the water
into a food processor and blend until
smooth. Alternatively, chop the onion
and celery very finely, then grind
with the garlic and herbs in a pestle
and mortar, gradually mixing in the
water. Pour into a pan and set aside.

2 Put the chopped coconut and liquid
into the food processor and mix to a
thick milk, adding water if necessary.
Alternatively, finely grate the coconut
and mix with the liquid. Add to the
onion and celery mixture in the pan.

3 Stir in the pigeon peas and
chilli and cook over a low heat for
15 minutes. Season to taste.

4 Put the oil and sugar in a heavy-
based casserole and cook over a
moderate heat until the sugar begins
to caramelize.

5 Add the chicken and cook for 15–20
minutes, turning frequently, until
browned all over.

6 Stir in the coconut mixture, the rice
and remaining water. Bring to the boil,
then reduce the heat, cover and
simmer for 20 minutes until the
chicken and rice are tender and the
liquid has been absorbed. Garnish
with celery leaves and serve.

Chicken & Vegetable Rice

Boneless chicken breasts may be used instead of the drumsticks, in which case slash them diagonally to allow the flavours of the sauce to penetrate.

Serves 4-6
4 chicken drumsticks
3 tbsp mango chutney
1 1/2 tbsp lemon juice
6 tbsp vegetable oil
1-2 tbsp medium or hot curry paste
1 1/2 tsp paprika
1 large onion, chopped
125 g/4 oz/1 1/2 cups button mushrooms
2 carrots, sliced thinly
2 celery sticks (stalks), trimmed and sliced thinly
1/2 aubergine (eggplant), quartered and sliced
2 garlic cloves, crushed
1/2 tsp ground cinnamon
250 g/8 oz/1 1/4 cups long-grain rice
600 ml/1 pint/2 1/2 cups chicken stock or water
60 g/2 oz/1/2 cup frozen peas or sliced French green beans
60 g/2 oz/1/3 cup seedless raisins
salt and pepper
wedges of hard-boiled (hard cooked) egg and lemon slices, to garnish (optional)

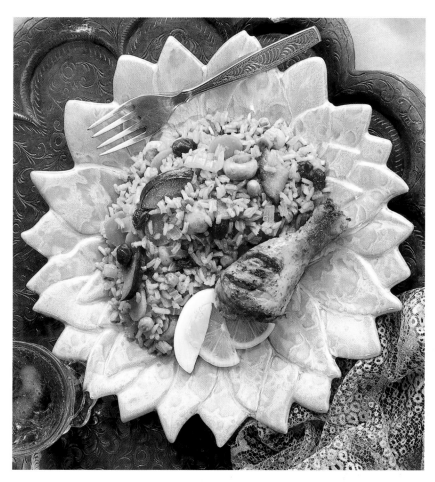

1 Slash the drumsticks twice on each side, cutting through the skin and deep into the flesh. Mix the chutney with the lemon juice, 1 tablespoon of the oil, the curry paste and paprika. Brush over the drumsticks and reserve the remainder.

2 Heat 2 tablespoons of oil in the frying pan (skillet) and fry the drumsticks for about 5 minutes until sealed and golden brown all over.

3 Meanwhile, heat the remaining oil. Add the onion, mushrooms, carrots, celery, aubergine (eggplant), garlic and cinnamon, and fry for 1 minute. Stir in the rice and cook for 1 minute. Stir to coat the rice with the oil. Add the stock and the remaining mango chutney mixture, peas and raisins. Mix and bring to the boil.

4 Reduce the heat and add the drumsticks to the mixture, pushing

them down into the liquid. Cover and cook gently for 25 minutes until the liquid is absorbed, the drumsticks are tender and the rice is cooked.

5 Transfer the rice to a warmed serving plate and arrange the drumsticks around it. Garnish the dish with wedges of hard-boiled (hard cooked) egg and lemon slices, if using.

Jambalaya

Jambalaya, New Orlean's paella, dates back to the 18th century, when it was served as slave food. Today, this hearty rice dish can contain any number of meats, such as chicken, duck, ham or sausage.

Serves 4
60 g/2 oz/¼ cup butter
2 onions, chopped
2 garlic cloves, crushed
5 celery sticks (stalks), chopped
1 red (bell) pepper, chopped
1 green (bell) pepper, chopped
1 tsp Cajun Spice Mixture (page 199)
250 g/8 oz/1 cup long-grain rice
425 g/14 oz can of tomatoes, drained and chopped
500 g/1 lb cooked assorted meats (chicken, duck, ham or sausage), sliced or diced
250 ml/8 fl oz/1 cup vegetable stock or white wine
1 tsp salt
parsley sprigs, to garnish

1 Melt the butter in a large, heavy-based pan. Add the onions, garlic, celery, (bell) peppers and spice mixture and mix well.

2 Add the rice and stir well to coat the grains in the butter mixture.

3 Add the tomatoes, meats, stock or wine and salt. Bring to the boil, stirring well.

4 Reduce the heat, cover and simmer for about 15 minutes or until the rice is cooked and fluffy and has absorbed all the liquid. If the mixture seems to be too dry then add a little boiling water, tablespoon by tablespoon, towards the end of the cooking time.

5 Serve the jamabalaya on warm plates, garnished with parsley.

Baton Rouge Chicken Gumbo

Everyone in the state of Louisiana, USA, has their own favourite gumbo recipe.
This one uses chicken with prawns (shrimp), okra and a little belly of pork:
a recipe that is hard to improve upon.

Serves 4–6
30 g/1 oz/2 tbsp butter
1 tbsp corn oil
30 g/1 oz/¼ cup plain (all-purpose) flour
90 g/3 oz belly pork, sliced
1 large onion, sliced
2 celery sticks (stalks), chopped
500 g/1 lb okra, trimmed and sliced
425 g/14 oz can peeled tomatoes
2 garlic cloves, crushed
1 litre/1¾ pints/4½ cups chicken stock or water
250 g/8 oz peeled prawns (shrimp)
500 g/1 lb cooked chicken, skinned and cut into bite-sized pieces
1 tsp Tabasco sauce
500 g/1 lb/3 cups hot cooked rice, to serve

4 Gradually add the stock to the browned roux, mixing and blending well, then add to the okra mixture. Cover and simmer for 1 hour.

5 Add the prawns (shrimp) and chicken to the okra mixture, cook for a further 5 minutes until the chicken is thoroughly reheated. Stir in the Tabasco.

6 Spoon the gumbo into individual serving bowls and top with a scoop of hot cooked rice.

1 Heat the butter and oil in a small, heavy-based pan. Add the flour and cook, stirring frequently, over a low heat until the roux turns a rich brown colour. Set aside.

2 Meanwhile, in a large pan, fry the pork slices gently, without extra fat, until they are golden brown on all sides and the fat has been rendered. Add the sliced onion and celery, and cook for a further 5 minutes.

3 Stir in the okra and fry gently for a further 3 minutes. Stir in the tomatoes and garlic, and simmer over gentle heat for 15 minutes.

Chicken Etouffé

Etouffé means smothered and is a popular way of presenting food in Cajun cuisine. Here, strips of chicken and vegetables are smothered in a thickened dark sauce flavoured with basil.

Serves 4–6
60 g/2 oz/¼ cup butter
1 small onion, chopped
1 celery stick (stalk), chopped
1 small green (bell) pepper, chopped
1 red (bell) pepper, cored, chopped
1 small red chilli, deseeded and finely chopped
1 tsp Cajun Spice Mixture (page 199)
1 tsp chopped fresh basil
2 tbsp vegetable oil
2 tbsp flour
475 ml/16 fl oz/2 cups rich chicken stock
500 g/1 lb skinless, boneless chicken breasts, cut into strips or bite-sized pieces
4 spring onions (scallions), chopped
salt
rice or couscous, to serve

1 Melt the butter in a large, heavy-based pan. Add the onion, celery, green and red (bell) peppers and chilli and cook over a gentle heat until softened, about 5 minutes.

2 Add the Cajun Spice Mixture, basil and salt. Cook for a further 2 minutes.

3 Meanwhile, heat the oil in a pan, add the flour and cook, slowly, until a rich red/brown roux is formed. Whisk constantly to prevent the roux from scorching and becoming bitter.

4 Gradually add the stock and whisk well to make a smooth thickened

sauce. Pour the sauce over the vegetable mixture and allow to simmer for about 15 minutes.

5 Add the chicken strips and the spring onions (scallions) and cook for

a further 10 minutes, stirring occasionally until the chicken is cooked and tender.

6 Serve with cooked long-grain rice or freshly cooked fluffy couscous.

Grillades with Grits

Grillades is a Cajun meat and vegetable stew in a thick gravy. It is considered to be Bayou breakfast food and would always be served with grits, a kind of creamy cereal (not unlike porridge) made from corn.

Serves 6
4 tbsp olive oil
1 kg/2 lb skinless, boneless chicken breasts, cut into 7 × 10 cm/3 × 4 inch strips
60 g/2 oz/$\frac{1}{2}$ cup plain (all-purpose) flour
3 onions, chopped
2 green (bell) peppers, chopped
4 celery sticks (stalks), finely chopped
1 garlic clove, crushed
3 medium ripe tomatoes, peeled, deseeded and chopped
2 tbsp tomato purée (paste)
1 tsp chopped fresh thyme
$\frac{1}{2}$–1 tsp Tabasco sauce
1$\frac{1}{2}$ tsp paprika
$\frac{1}{4}$ tsp cayenne pepper
1 tsp salt
150 ml/1$\frac{1}{4}$ pint/$\frac{2}{3}$ cup vegetable stock
150 ml/$\frac{1}{4}$ pint/$\frac{2}{3}$ cup white wine
grits hominy or couscous, to serve

1 Heat the oil in a heavy-based frying pan (skillet). Add the chicken strips and fry quickly on both sides until no longer pink and they are sealed all over. Remove with perforated spoon and set aside.

2 Add the flour to the pan juices and mix well, stirring until the flour is absorbed by the juices. Cook over a gentle heat, stirring constantly, until the roux changes to a rich brown colour.

3 Add the onions, (bell) peppers, celery and garlic, and mix. Cover and cook over a gentle heat for 15 minutes.

4 Return the meat to the pan with the tomatoes, tomato purée (paste), thyme, Tabasco sauce, paprika, cayenne, salt, stock and wine, mixing well.

5 Cover and simmer gently for a further 40–45 minutes, or until the chicken and vegetables are cooked.

6 Serve hot with grits or couscous.

Bourguignonne of Chicken

A recipe based on a classic French dish. Use a good quality wine
when making this casserole.

Serves 4–6
4 tbsp sunflower oil
900 g/1³/₄ lb chicken meat, diced
250 g/8 oz/3 cups button mushrooms
125 g/4 oz/²/₃ cup rindless, smoked bacon, diced
16 shallots
2 garlic cloves, crushed
1 tbsp plain (all-purpose) flour
150ml/¹/₄ pint/²/₃ cup white Burgundy wine
150ml/¹/₄ pint/²/₃ cup chicken stock
1 bouquet garni (1 bay leaf, sprig thyme, stick of celery, parsley and sage tied with string)
salt and pepper

1 Heat the sunflower oil in an ovenproof casserole and brown the chicken all over, remove from the casserole with a slotted spoon.

2 Add the mushrooms, bacon, shallots and garlic to the casserole and cook for 4 minutes.

3 Return the chicken to the casserole and sprinkle with flour. Cook for a further 2 minutes.

4 Add the wine and stock and stir until boiling. Add the bouquet garni and season well with salt and pepper.

5 Cover the casserole and bake in the centre of a preheated oven, 150°C/300°F/Gas Mark 2, for 1½ hours. Remove the bouquet garni.

6 Deep fry some heart-shaped croûtons (about 8 large ones) in beef dripping and serve with the bourguignonne.

COOK'S TIP

A good quality red wine can be used instead of the white wine, to produce a rich, glossy red sauce.

Spiced Chicken Casserole

Spices, herbs, fruit, nuts and vegetables are combined to make an appealing casserole with lots of flavour.

Serves 4–6
3 tbsp olive oil
900 g/1³/₄ lb chicken meat, sliced
10 shallots or pickling onions
3 carrots, chopped
60 g/2 oz/¹/₂ cup chestnuts, sliced
60 g/2 oz/¹/₂ cup flaked almonds, toasted
1 tsp freshly grated nutmeg
3 tsp ground cinnamon
300 ml/¹/₂ pint/1¹/₄ cups white wine
300 ml/¹/₂ pint/1¹/₄ cups chicken stock
175 ml/ 6fl oz/³/₄ cup white wine vinegar
1 tbsp chopped fresh tarragon
1 tbsp chopped fresh flat leaf parsley
1 tbsp chopped fresh thyme
grated rind of 1 orange
1 tbsp dark muscovado sugar
125 g/4 oz/³/₄ cup seedless black grapes, halved
sea salt and pepper
fresh herbs, to garnish

1 Heat the olive oil in a large saucepan and fry the chicken, shallots and carrots for about 6 minutes until browned.

2 Add the remaining ingredients, except the grapes, and simmer over a low heat for 2 hours until the meat is very tender.

3 Add the grapes just before serving and serve with wild rice or puréed potato. Garnish with herbs.

Hungarian Chicken Goulash

Goulash is traditionally made with beef, but this recipe successfully uses chicken instead. To reduce fat, use a low-fat cream in place of the soured cream.

Serves 6
900 g/1¾ lb chicken meat, diced
60 g/2 oz/½ cup flour, seasoned with 1 tsp paprika, salt and pepper
2 tbsp olive oil
30 g/1 oz/2 tbsp butter
1 onion, sliced
24 shallots, peeled
1 each red and green (bell) pepper, chopped
1 tbsp paprika
1 tsp rosemary, crushed
4 tbsp tomato purée (paste)
300 ml/½ pint/1¼ cups chicken stock
150 ml/¼ pint/⅔ cup claret
425 g/14 oz can chopped tomatoes
150ml/¼ pint/⅔ cup soured cream
1 tbsp chopped fresh parsley, to garnish

1 Toss the meat into the seasoned flour until coated all over.

2 In a flameproof casserole, heat the oil and butter and fry the onion, shallots and peppers for 3 minutes.

3 Add the chicken and cook for a further 4 minutes.

4 Sprinkle with the paprika and rosemary.

5 Add the tomato purée (paste), chicken stock, claret and chopped tomatoes, cover and cook in the centre of a preheated oven, 160°C/325°F/Gas Mark 3 for 1½ hours.

6 Remove the casserole from the oven, allow it to stand for 4 minutes, then add the soured cream and garnish with parsley.

7 Serve with chunks of bread and a side salad.

COOK'S VARIATION

Serve the goulash with buttered ribbon noodles instead of bread. For an authentic touch, try a Hungarian red wine instead of the claret.

Chicken with Shallots in Wild Mushroom & Ginger Sauce

This recipe has an oriental flavour, which can be further enhanced with chopped spring onions, cinnamon and lemon grass.

Serves 6–8
6 tbsp sesame oil
900 g/1³/₄ lb chicken meat
60 g/2 oz/¹/₂ cup flour, seasoned
32 shallots, sliced
500 g/1 lb/6 cups wild mushrooms, roughly chopped
300 ml/¹/₂ pint/1¹/₄ cups chicken stock
2 tbsp Worcestershire sauce
1 tbsp honey
2 tbsp grated fresh root ginger
150 ml/¹/₄ pint/²/₃ cup yogurt
salt and pepper
flat leaf parsley, to garnish

1 Heat the oil in a large frying pan. Coat the chicken in the seasoned flour and cook for about 4 minutes, until browned all over. Transfer to a large deep casserole.

2 Slowly fry the shallots and mushrooms in the juices.

3 Add the chicken stock, Worcestershire sauce, honey and fresh ginger, then season to taste with salt and pepper.

4 Pour the mixture over the chicken, and cover the casserole with a lid or cooking foil.

5 Cook in the centre of a preheated oven, 150°C/300°F/Gas Mark 2, for 1¹/₂ hours until the meat is very tender. Add the yogurt and cook for a further 10 minutes. Serve with a mixture of wild rice and white rice, and garnish with parsley.

Fricasseé of Chicken in Lime Sauce

The addition of lime juice and lime rind adds a delicious tangy
flavour to this chicken stew.

Serves 4
2 tbsp oil
1 large chicken, cut into small portions
60 g/2 oz/^{1}/$_2$ cup flour, seasoned
500 g/1 lb baby onions or shallots, sliced
1 each green and red (bell) pepper, sliced thinly
150 ml/^{1}/$_4$ pint/^{2}/$_3$ cup chicken stock
juice and rind of 2 limes
2 chillies, chopped
2 tbsp oyster sauce
1 tsp Worcestershire sauce
salt and pepper

1 Heat the oil in a large frying pan. Coat the chicken pieces in the seasoned flour and cook for about 4 minutes until browned all over.

2 Transfer the chicken to a large, deep casserole and sprinkle with the sliced onions.

3 Slowly fry the peppers in the juices in the frying pan.

4 Add the chicken stock, lime juice and rind and cook for a further 5 minutes.

5 Add the chillies, oyster sauce and Worcestershire sauce. Season to taste.

6 Pour the peppers and juices over the chicken and onions.

7 Cover the casserole with a lid or cooking foil.

8 Cook in the centre of a preheated oven, 190°C/375°F/Gas Mark 5, for 1½ hours until the chicken is very tender, then serve.

COOK'S TIP

Try this casserole with a cheese scone (biscuit) topping. About 30 minutes before the end of cooking time, simply top with rounds cut from cheese scone (biscuit) pastry.

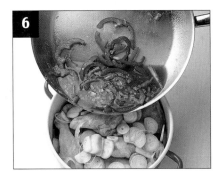

Brittany Chicken Casserole

A hearty, one-dish meal that would make a substantial lunch or supper.

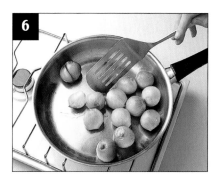

Serves 6

500 g/1 lb/2¹/₂ cups beans,
such as flageolets,
soaked overnight and drained
30 g/1 oz/2 tbsp butter
2 tbsp olive oil
3 rindless bacon slices, chopped
900 g/1³/₄ lb chicken pieces
1 tbsp plain (all-purpose) flour
300 ml/¹/₂ pint/1¹/₄ cups cider
150 ml/¹/₄ pint/²/₃ cup
chicken stock
14 shallots
2 tbsp honey, warmed
250 g/8 oz ready-cooked beetroot
salt and pepper

1 Cook the beans in salted boiling water for about 25 minutes.

2 Heat the butter and olive oil in a flameproof casserole, add the bacon and chicken and cook for 5 minutes.

3 Sprinkle with flour then add the cider and chicken stock. Mix well, season and bring to the boil.

4 Add the beans, cover tightly with a lid or cooking foil and bake in the centre of a preheated oven, 160°C/325°F/Gas Mark 3, for 2 hours.

5 About 15 minutes before the end of cooking time, remove the lid or cooking foil from the casserole.

6 Gently cook the shallots and honey together in a frying for 5 minutes.

7 Add the shallots and cooked beetroot to the casserole and leave to finish cooking in the oven for the last 15 minutes.

COOK'S TIP

To save time, use canned flageolet beans instead of dried. Drain and rinse before adding to the chicken.

Chicken Madeira "French-style"

Madeira adds a rich, full flavour to this casserole dish.

Serves 8
30 g/1 oz/2 tbsp butter
20 baby onions
280 g/9 oz/1$^1/_2$ cups carrots, sliced
280 g/9 oz/1$^1/_2$ cups bacon, chopped
280 g/9 oz/3 cups button mushrooms
1 chicken, weighing about 1.5 kg/3 lb
425 ml/15 fl oz/1$^7/_8$ cups white wine
30 g/1 oz/$^1/_4$ cup seasoned flour
425ml/15 fl oz/1$^7/_8$ cups chicken stock
bouquet garni
150 ml/$^1/_4$ pint/$^2/_3$ cup Madeira wine
salt and pepper

1 Heat the butter in a large frying pan and fry the onions, carrots, bacon and mushrooms for 3 minutes.Transfer to a large casserole dish.

2 Add the chicken to the frying pan and brown all over. Transfer to the casserole dish with the vegetables and bacon.

3 Add the wine and cook until the wine is nearly completely reduced.

4 Sprinkle with the seasoned flour.

5 Add the chicken stock, salt and pepper and the bouquet garni. Cover and cook for 2 hours. About 30 minutes before the end of cooking time, add the Madeira and cook uncovered.

6 Carve the chicken and serve with mashed potato or pasta.

Garlic Chicken Cassoulet

This is a cassoulet with a twist – it is made with chicken instead of duck and lamb.
Save time by using canned beans, such as borlotti or cannellini beans,
which are both good in this dish.

Serves 4
4 tbsp sunflower oil
900 g/1¾ lb chicken meat, chopped
250 g/8 oz/3 cups mushrooms, sliced
16 shallots
6 garlic cloves, crushed
1 tbsp plain (all-purpose) flour
250 ml/8 fl oz/1 cup white wine
250 ml/8 fl oz/1 cup chicken stock
1 bouquet garni (1 bay leaf, sprig thyme, celery, parsley & sage tied with string)
425 g/14 oz can borlotti beans
salt and pepper

1 Heat the sunflower oil in an ovenproof casserole and fry the chicken until browned all over. Remove from the casserole with a slotted spoon.

2 Add the mushrooms, shallots and garlic to the fat in the casserole and cook for 4 minutes.

3 Return the chicken to the casserole and sprinkle with the flour then cook for a further 2 minutes.

4 Add the wine and stock, stir until boiling then add the bouquet garni. Season well with salt and pepper.

5 Stir in the borlotti beans.

6 Cover and place in the centre of a preheated oven, 150°C/300°F/Gas Mark 2, for 2 hours. Remove the bouquet garni and serve.

Country Chicken Braise with Rosemary Dumplings

Root vegetables are always cheap and nutritious, and combined with chicken they make tasty and economical casseroles.

Serves 4
4 chicken quarters
2 tbsp sunflower oil
2 medium leeks
250 g/8 oz/1 cup carrots, chopped
250 g/8 oz/2 cups parsnips, chopped
2 small turnips, chopped
600 ml/1 pint/2^1/$_2$ cups chicken stock
3 tbsp Worcestershire sauce
2 sprigs fresh rosemary
salt and pepper

DUMPLINGS

200 g/7 oz/1^3/$_4$ cups self-raising (self-rising) flour
105 g/3^1/$_2$ oz shredded suet
1 tbsp chopped rosemary leaves
cold water, to mix

1 Remove the skin from the chicken if you prefer. Heat the oil in a large, flameproof casserole or heavy pan and fry the chicken until golden. Remove from the pan. Drain off the excess fat.

2 Trim and slice the leeks. Add the carrots, parsnips and turnips to the casserole and cook for 5 minutes, until lightly coloured. Return the chicken to the pan.

3 Add the stock, Worcestershire sauce, rosemary and seasoning, then bring to the boil.

4 Reduce the heat, cover and simmer gently for about 50 minutes or until the chicken juices run clear when the chicken is pierced with a skewer.

5 To make the dumplings, combine the flour, suet and rosemary leaves with salt and pepper in a bowl. Stir in just enough cold water to bind to a firm dough.

6 Form into eight small balls and place on top of the chicken and vegetables. Cover and simmer for a further 10–12 minutes, until the dumplings are well risen.

Rustic Chicken & Orange Pot

Low in fat and high in fibre, this colourful casserole
makes a healthy and hearty meal.

Serves 4
8 chicken drumsticks, skinned
1 tbsp wholemeal (whole wheat) flour
1 tbsp olive oil
2 medium red onions
1 garlic clove, crushed
1 tsp fennel seeds
1 bay leaf
finely grated rind and juice of 1 small orange
425 g/14 oz can chopped tomatoes
425 g/14 oz can cannellini or flageolet beans, drained
salt and black pepper

TOPPING
3 thick slices wholemeal (whole wheat) bread
2 tsp olive oil

1 Toss the chicken drumsticks in the flour to coat evenly. Heat the oil in a non-stick or heavy pan and fry the chicken over a fairly high heat, turning often until golden brown. Transfer to a large ovenproof casserole.

2 Slice the red onions into thin wedges. Add to the pan and cook for a few minutes until lightly browned. Stir in the garlic, then add the onions and garlic to the casserole.

3 Add the fennel seeds, bay leaf, orange rind and juice, tomatoes, beans and salt and pepper.

4 Cover tightly and cook in a preheated oven, 190°C/375°F/Gas Mark 5, for 30–35 minutes until the chicken juices are clear and not pink when pierced through the thickest part with a skewer.

5 For the topping, cut the bread into small dice and toss in the oil. Remove the lid from the casserole and top with the bread cubes. Bake for a further 15–20 minutes until the bread is golden and crisp. Serve hot.

Rich Mediterranean Chicken Casserole

A colourful casserole packed with sunshine flavours from the Mediterranean. Sun-dried tomatoes add a wonderful richness and you need very few to make this dish really special.

Serves 4

8 chicken thighs

2 tbsp olive oil

1 medium red onion, sliced

2 garlic cloves, crushed

1 large red pepper,
sliced thickly

thinly pared rind and juice
of 1 small orange

120 ml/4 floz/^{1}/$_2$ cup
chicken stock

425 g/14 oz can chopped
tomatoes

25 g/1 oz/^{1}/$_2$ cup sun-dried
tomatoes, thinly sliced

1 tbsp chopped fresh thyme

50 g/2 oz/^{1}/$_2$ cup pitted
black olives

salt and pepper

thyme sprigs and orange
rind, to garnish

1 In a heavy or non-stick large pan, fry the chicken without fat over a fairly high heat, turning occasionally until golden brown. Drain off any excess fat from the chicken and transfer to a flameproof casserole.

2 Fry the onion, garlic and pepper in the pan over a moderate heat for 3–4 minutes. Transfer to the casserole.

3 Add the orange rind and juice, chicken stock, canned tomatoes and sun-dried tomatoes.

4 Bring to the boil then cover with a lid and simmer very gently over a low heat for about 1 hour, stirring

occasionally. Add the thyme and olives, then adjust the seasoning with salt and pepper.

5 Scatter orange rind and thyme over the casserole to garnish, and serve with crusty bread.

COOK'S TIP

Sun-dried tomatoes have a dense texture and concentrated taste, and add intense flavour to slow-cooking casseroles.

Old English Chicken Stewed in Ale

A slow-cooked, old-fashioned stew to warm up a wintry day.
The rarebit toasts are a perfect accompaniment to soak up the rich juices,
but if you prefer, serve the stew with jacket potatoes.

Serves 4–6
4 large, skinless chicken thighs
2 tbsp plain (all-purpose) flour
2 tbsp English mustard powder
2 tbsp sunflower oil
15 g/$^{1}/_{2}$ oz/1 tbsp butter
4 small onions
600 ml/1 pint/2$^{1}/_{2}$ cups beer
2 tbsp Worcestershire sauce
3 tbsp chopped fresh sage leaves
salt and pepper

FOR THE RAREBIT TOASTS

60 g/2 oz/$^{1}/_{2}$ cup grated mature English Cheddar
1 tsp English mustard powder
1 tsp plain (all-purpose) flour
1 tsp Worcestershire sauce
1 tbsp beer
2 slices wholemeal (whole wheat) toast

1 Trim any excess fat from the chcken and toss in the flour and mustard to coat evenly. Heat the oil and butter in a large flameproof casserole and fry the chicken over a fairly high heat, turning occasionally until golden. Remove and keep hot.

2 Peel and slice the onions into wedges and fry quickly until golden. Add the chicken, beer, Worcestershire sauce, and salt and pepper. Bring to the boil, cover and simmer very gently for about 1½ hours, until the chicken is very tender.

3 Meanwhile, make the rarebit toasts: mix the cheese with the mustard, flour, Worcestershire sauce and beer. Spread over the toasts and place under a hot grill (broiler) for about 1 minute, until melted and golden. Cut into triangles.

4 Stir the sage into the chicken stew, bring to the boil and serve with the rarebit toasts, a green vegetable and new potatoes.

Jamaican Hot Pot

A tasty way to make chicken joints go a long way, this hearty casserole, spiced with the warm, subtle flavour of ginger, is a good choice for a Halloween party. If squash or pumpkin is not available, swede makes a good substitute.

Serves 4
2 tsp sunflower oil
4 chicken drumsticks
4 chicken thighs
1 medium onion
750 g/1$\frac{1}{2}$ lb piece squash or pumpkin, diced
1 green (bell) pepper, sliced
2.5 cm/1 inch fresh ginger root, chopped finely
425 g/14 oz can chopped tomatoes
300ml/$\frac{1}{2}$ pint/1$\frac{1}{4}$ cups chicken stock
60 g/2 oz/$\frac{1}{4}$ cup split lentils
garlic salt and cayenne pepper
350 g/12 oz can sweetcorn (corn-on-the-cob)

1 Heat the oil in a large flameproof casserole and fry the chicken joints until golden, turning frequently.

2 Peel and slice the onion.

3 Peel and slice the squash or pumpkin.

4 Deseed and slice the (bell) pepper.

5 Drain excess fat from the pan and add the onion, pumpkin and pepper. Gently fry for a few minutes until lightly browned. Add the ginger, tomatoes, stock and lentils. Season lightly with garlic salt and cayenne.

6 Cover and place in a preheated oven, 190°C/375°F/Gas Mark 5, for about 1 hour, until the vegetables are tender and the juices from the chicken run clear. Add the drained corn and cook for a further 5 minutes. Season to taste and serve with crusty bread.

COOK'S VARIATION

If you can't find fresh ginger root, add 1 teaspoon allspice for a warm, fragrant aroma.

Springtime Chicken Cobbler

Fresh spring vegetables are the basis of this colourful casserole, which is topped with hearty wholemeal (whole wheat) dumplings for a complete, healthy family meal. Vary the vegetables depending on what's available.

Serves 4
8 skinless chicken drumsticks
1 tbsp oil
1 small onion, sliced
350 g/12 oz/1½ cups baby carrots
2 baby turnips
125 g/4 oz/1 cup broad beans or peas
1 tsp cornflour
300ml/½ pint/1¼ cups chicken stock
2 bay leaves
salt and pepper

COBBLER TOPPING
250 g/8 oz/2 cups wholemeal (whole wheat) plain flour
2 tsp baking powder
30 g/1 oz/2 tbsp sunflower soft margarine
2 tsp dry wholegrain mustard
60 g/2 oz/½ cup Cheddar cheese, grated
skimmed milk, to mix
sesame seeds, to sprinkle

1 Fry the chicken in the oil, turning , until golden brown. Drain well and place in an ovenproof casserole. Sauté the onion for 2–3 minutes to soften.

2 Wash and trim the carrots and turnips and cut into equal-sized pieces. Add to the casserole with the onions and beans or peas.

3 Blend the cornflour with a little of the stock, then stir in the rest and heat gently, stirring until boiling. Pour into the casserole and add the bay leaves, salt and pepper.

4 Cover tightly and bake in a preheated oven, 200°C/400°F/Gas

Mark 6, for 50–60 minutes, or until the chicken juices run clear when pierced with a skewer.

5 For the topping, sift the flour and baking powder. Mix in the margarine with a fork. Stir in the mustard, the cheese and enough milk to mix to a fairly soft dough.

6 Roll out and cut 16 rounds with a 4 cm/1½ inch cutter.Uncover the casserole, arrange the scone (biscuit) rounds on top, then brush with milk and sprinkle with sesame seeds. Bake in the oven for 20 minutes or until the topping is golden and firm.

Country Chicken Hot-Pot

There are many regional versions of hot-pot, all using fresh, local ingredients Now, there are an endless variety of ingredients available all year perfect for traditional one-pot cooking. Hot-pots are always cooked slowly for a long time, allowing the rich flavours to permeate the chicken.

Serves 4
4 chicken quarters
6 medium potatoes, cut into 5mm/¼ inch slices
2 sprigs thyme
2 sprigs rosemary
2 bay leaves
200 g/7 oz/1 cup smoked streaky bacon, rinded and diced
1 large onion, chopped finely
200 g/7 oz/1 cup sliced carrots
150 ml/¼ pint/⅔ cup stout
30 g/1 oz/2 tbsp melted butter

1 Remove the skin from the chicken quarters if preferred.

2 Arrange a layer of potatoes in the bottom of a wide casserole. Season well, then add the herbs.

3 Top with the chicken quarters, then sprinkle with the diced bacon, onion and carrots. Season well and arrange the remaining potatoes on top, overlapping slightly.

4 Pour over the stout, brush the potatoes with the melted butter and cover with a lid.

5 Bake in a preheated oven, 150°C/300°F/Gas Mark 2, for about 2 hours, uncovering for the last 30 minutes to allow the potatoes to brown. Serve hot, with fresh seasonal vegetables.

Country Chicken Bake

This economical bake is a complete meal to cook and serve in one pot – and it's easy to adjust for any amount of servings. Its crusty, herb-flavoured French bread topping mops up the tasty juices, and means there's no need to serve potatoes or rice separately.

Serves 4
2 tbsp sunflower oil
4 chicken quarters
16 small whole onions, peeled
3 sticks (stalks) celery, sliced
425 g/14 oz can red kidney beans
4 medium tomatoes, quartered
200 ml/7floz/ scant 1 cup dry cider or stock
4 tbsp chopped fresh parsley
1 tsp paprika
60 g/2 oz/4 tbsp butter
12 slices French bread
salt and pepper

1 Heat the oil in a flameproof casserole and fry the chicken quarters two at a time until golden. Remove from the pan and set aside.

2 Add the onions, turning occasionally, until golden brown. Add the celery and fry for 2–3 minutes. then stir in the beans, tomatoes, cider, half the parsley, salt and pepper. Sprinkle with the paprika.

3 Return the chicken to the pan and stir in the beans, tomatoes, cider, half the parsley and salt and pepper. Sprinkle with the paprika. Cover and cook in a preheated oven, 200°C/400°F/Gas Mark 6, for 20–25 minutes, until the chicken juices run clear when pierced with a skewer.

4 Mix the remaining parsley with the butter and spread evenly over the French bread.

5 Uncover the casserole, arrange the bread slices overlapping on top and bake for a further 10–12 minutes, until golden and crisp.

COOK'S TIP

Add a crushed garlic clove to the parsley butter for extra flavour.

Quick Chicken Dishes

One of the marvellous qualities of chicken is that when cut into small pieces, it can be cooked very quickly, which is welcome for those of us who are too busy to spend a lot of time preparing meals. In this section, you can select a tasty nutritious dish that won't take hours to make. Pasta makes a perfect partner for chicken as it is also quick to cook. Look for Pasta Medley and Italian

Chicken Spirals. Smaller cuts of chicken are also ideal for stir-fries that can be quickly cooked to produce tender, moist and flavourful chicken. Speedy Peanut Pan-fry is a crunchy stir-fry that is served with noodles, while Chicken & Almond Rissoles with Stir-fried Vegetables offers chicken and potato rissoles with a nutty coating that are served with a colourful mixture of crunchy flash-cooked vegetables.

Chicken with Lemon & Tarragon

Chicken fillets are cooked with saffron, white wine and stock flavoured
with lemon rind and tarragon, then the sauce is thickened with
egg yolks and soured cream and finished with mayonnaise.

Serves 6
6 large skinless, boneless chicken breasts
1/4 tsp saffron strands
250 ml/8 fl oz/1 cup boiling water
1 tbsp olive oil
30 g/1 oz/2 tbsp butter
1 garlic clove, crushed
120 ml/4 fl oz/1/2 cup dry white wine
grated rind of 1 small lemon
1 tbsp lemon juice
1–2 tbsp chopped fresh tarragon
2 tsp cornflour (cornstarch)
1 egg yolk
6 tbsp soured cream
or double (heavy) cream
4 tbsp thick mayonnaise
salt and pepper

TO GARNISH

sprigs of fresh tarragon
lemon twists

1 Cut each chicken breast almost
horizontally into three thin slices
with a sharp knife. Season each piece
well with salt and pepper.

2 Put the saffron strands into a bowl,
pour on the boiling water and leave to
stand until needed.

3 Heat the oil, butter and garlic in a
frying pan (skillet). When foaming,
add the chicken and fry on each side
until lightly coloured.

4 Add the saffron liquid, wine, lemon
rind and juice, and half the tarragon.
Bring to the boil, then simmer for
about 5 minutes until tender.

5 Remove the chicken with a
perforated spoon and place on a
serving dish in overlapping slices.
Leave to cool. Boil the remaining
juices in the pan for 3–4 minutes to
reduce slightly.

6 Blend the cornflour (cornstarch),
egg yolk and cream together in a bowl.
Whisk in a little of the cooking juices,
then return to the pan and heat

gently, stirring continuously until
thickened and just barely simmering.
Remove from the heat, adjust the
seasoning and pour into a bowl. Cover
and leave until cool.

7 Beat the mayonnaise and remaining
fresh tarragon into the sauce and
spoon over the chicken. Cover and
chill thoroughly. Garnish with sprigs
of fresh tarragon and lemon twists.

Pasta Medley

Strips of cooked chicken are tossed with coloured pasta, grapes and carrot sticks in a pesto-flavoured dressing. Any leftovers can be kept in the refrigerator for a day or two.

Serves 2
125–150 g/4–5 oz dried pasta shapes, such as twists or bows
1 tbsp oil
2 tbsp mayonnaise
2 tsp bottled pesto sauce
1 tbsp soured cream or natural fromage frais
175 g/6 oz cooked skinless, boneless chicken meat
1–2 celery sticks (stalks)
125 g/4 oz/1 cup black grapes (preferably seedless)
1 large carrot, trimmed
salt and pepper
celery leaves, to garnish
FRENCH DRESSING
1 tbsp wine vinegar
3 tbsp extra-virgin olive oil
salt and pepper

1 To make the French dressing, whisk all the ingredients together until smooth.

2 Cook the pasta with the oil for about 12 minutes in plenty of boiling, salted water until just tender. Drain thoroughly, rinse and drain again. Transfer to a bowl and mix in 1 tablespoon of the French dressing while hot; leave until cold.

3 Combine the mayonnaise, pesto sauce and soured cream or fromage frais in a bowl, and season to taste.

4 Cut the chicken into narrow strips. Cut the celery diagonally into narrow

slices. Reserve a few grapes for garnish, halve the rest and remove any pips (seeds). Cut the carrot into narrow julienne strips.

5 Add the chicken, the celery, the halved grapes, the carrot and the mayonnaise mixture to the pasta, and toss thoroughly. Check the seasoning, adding more salt and pepper if necessary.

6 Arrange the pasta medley on two plates and garnish with the reserved black grapes and the celery leaves.

Tagliatelle with Chicken & Almonds

Spinach tagliatelle with a rich tomato sauce and creamy
chicken makes a very appetizing dish.

Serves 4
60 g/2 oz/¹/₄ cup unsalted butter
425 g/14 oz skinless, boneless chicken breasts, sliced thinly
90 g/3 oz/³/₄ cup blanched almonds
300 ml/¹/₂ pint/1¹/₄ cups double (heavy) cream
250 g/8 oz fresh green ribbon noodles
salt and pepper
basil leaves, to garnish

TOMATO SAUCE

1 small onion, chopped
2 tbsp olive oil
1 garlic clove, chopped
425 g/14 oz can of chopped tomatoes
2 tbsp chopped fresh parsley
1 tsp dried oregano
2 bay leaves
2 tbsp tomato purée (paste)
1 tsp sugar

1 To make the tomato sauce, fry the onion gently in the oil until translucent. Add the garlic and fry for 1 minute further. Stir in the remaining ingredients and bring to the boil. Simmer, uncovered, for 15–20 minutes until reduced by half. Discard the bay leaves and keep the sauce warm.

2 Melt the butter and fry the chicken and almonds gently in a pan for 5–6 minutes, stirring frequently.

3 Meanwhile, boil the cream in a small pan for about 10 minutes, until reduced by almost half.

4 Stir the cream into the chicken mixture and season with salt and pepper. Set aside and keep warm.

5 Cook the pasta in a large pan of boiling salted water until just tender.

Drain the pasta and turn into a warmed serving dish.

6 Spoon the tomato sauce over the pasta with the chicken mixture in the centre. Garnish with basil and serve.

Tortellini

According to legend, tortellini are said
to resemble Venus's tummy button.

Serves 4
125 g/4 oz cooked skinless, boneless chicken breasts, chopped
60 g/2 oz/¹/₃ cup Parma ham
45 g/1¹/₂ oz cooked drained spinach
1 tbsp finely chopped onion
2 tbsp grated Parmesan
good pinch of ground allspice
1 egg, beaten
salt and pepper

PASTA DOUGH

pinch of salt
325 g/11 oz/generous 2¹/₂ cups flour
3 large eggs
1 tbsp each olive oil & water

SAUCE

300 ml/¹/₂ pint/1¹/₄ cups single (light) cream
1–2 garlic cloves, crushed
125 g/4 oz/1¹/₂ cups mushrooms, thinly sliced
4 tbsp freshly grated Parmesan
1–2 tbsp chopped fresh parsley
salt and pepper

1 To make the pasta dough, sift the flour and salt on to a flat surface. Make a well in the centre. Beat the eggs, oil and water together, pour into the well and work together to form a dough. Knead for 10–15 minutes. Cover with a damp cloth and leave for 10–15 minutes.

2 Process the chicken with the Parma ham, spinach and onion, until finely chopped. Add the Parmesan, allspice, seasoning and egg.

3 Roll out the dough, half at a time, very thinly. Cut into 4 cm/1¹/₂ inch rounds. Place ¹/₂ teaspoon of the filling on each. Fold into a semi-circle and seal the edges. Wrap the semi-circle round your finger, crossing the ends. Press together and curl the rest of the dough back. Place on a floured tray. Repeat with the rest of the dough.

4 Cook in batches. Once they rise to the surface, cook for 5 minutes. Drain, keep warm, and cook the remainder. For the sauce, heat the cream and garlic and bring to the boil. Add the mushrooms and half the Parmesan. Simmer for 2 minutes. Add the parsley and pour over the pasta. Sprinkle with the remaining Parmesan and serve.

Chicken Kiev

This classic dish from the Ukraine is delicious
served with sautéed potatoes.

Serves 4
1 garlic clove, crushed
90 g/3 oz/$^1/_3$ cup butter
4 skinless, boneless chicken breasts
oil for deep-frying
125 g/4 oz/1 cup plain (all-purpose) flour
2 eggs, beaten
2 tbsp milk
breadcrumbs, for coating
salt and pepper
TO GARNISH
chopped parsley
lemon wedges

1 Mash the garlic into the butter with a fork. Season well and shape into a square patty. Put into the freezer while you prepare the chicken.

2 Slice each chicken breast horizontally in half, and lay between sheets of clingfilm (plastic wrap). Flatten each piece to even thickness. Discard the clingfilm (plastic wrap).

3 When the butter is quite hard, cut it into four batons. Place a baton lengthways on four of the chicken breast slices. Cover each with another breast slice and refrigerate until ready to serve.

4 Beat the eggs and milk together. When ready to serve, add oil to a pan to a depth of about 5 cm/2 inches and heat to a moderate, deep-frying temperature, 190°C/375°F. Coat each

Kiev with flour, then the egg mixture, and finally with breadcrumbs. Repeat once to form a good seal. Fry each Kiev for about 5 minutes. Serve at once while still piping hot.

COOK'S TIP

About 1 tablespoon chopped fresh parsley can be added to the garlic and butter.

Chicken & Almond Rissoles with Stir-fried Vegetables

Cooked potatoes and cooked chicken are combined to make tasty rissoles rolled in chopped almonds then served with stir-fried vegetables.

Serves 1
125 g/4 oz boiled potatoes
90 g/3 oz/$\frac{1}{2}$ cup carrots
125 g/4 oz/1 cup cooked chicken meat
1 garlic clove, crushed
$\frac{1}{2}$ tsp dried tarragon or thyme
generous pinch of ground allspice or ground coriander seeds
1 egg yolk, or $\frac{1}{2}$ egg, beaten
about 30 g/1 oz/$\frac{1}{4}$ cup flaked (slivered) almonds
salt and pepper

STIR-FRIED VEGETABLES

1 celery stick (stalk)
2 spring onions (scallions), trimmed
1 tbsp oil
8 baby sweetcorn cobs (corn-on-the-cob)
about 10–12 mangetout (snow peas) or sugar snap peas, trimmed
2 tsp balsamic vinegar
salt and pepper

1 Grate the boiled potatoes and raw carrots coarsely into a bowl. Chop finely or mince (grind) the chicken and add to the vegetables with the garlic, tarragon, allspice or coriander and plenty of salt and pepper.

2 Add the egg yolk or beaten egg and bind the ingredients together. Divide in half and shape into sausages.

3 Chop the almonds evenly and then roll each rissole in the nuts until evenly coated.

4 Place the rissoles in a greased ovenproof dish and cook in a

preheated oven, 200°C/400°F/Gas Mark 6, for about 20 minutes or until lightly browned; alternatively, fry in a little oil until browned all over and cooked through.

5 While the rissoles cook, prepare the stir-fried vegetables. Cut the celery and spring onions (scallions) on the diagonal into narrow slices. Heat the oil in a frying pan (skillet) and toss in the vegetables. Cook over a high heat for 1–2 minutes, then add the sweetcorn cobs and peas, and cook for 2–3 minutes. Finally, add the balsamic vinegar and season with salt and pepper to taste.

6 Spoon the stir-fried vegetables on to a serving plate and place the rissoles beside them. Serve at once.

Chicken with Peanut Sauce

A tangy stir-fry with a strong peanut flavour.
Serve with freshly boiled rice or noodles.

Serves 4
4 skinless, boneless chicken breasts, weighing 625 g/1¼ lb
4 tbsp soy sauce
4 tbsp sherry
3 tbsp crunchy peanut butter
350 g/12 oz courgettes (zucchini), trimmed
2 tbsp sunflower oil
4–6 spring onions (scallions), thinly sliced diagonally
250 g/8 oz can of bamboo shoots, well drained and sliced
salt and pepper
4 tbsp desiccated (shredded) coconut, toasted, to garnish

6 Add the peanut butter mixture and heat thoroughly, stirring all the time so everything is coated in the sauce as it thickens. Adjust the seasoning and serve very hot, sprinkled with the toasted coconut.

COOK'S TIP

If you prefer, smooth peanut butter can be used instead of the crunchy variety.

1 Cut the chicken into thin strips across the grain and season lightly with salt and pepper.

2 Put the soy sauce in a bowl with the sherry and peanut butter, and stir until smooth and well blended.

3 Cut the courgettes (zucchini) into 5 cm/2 inch lengths and then cut into sticks about 5 mm/¼ inch thick.

4 Heat the oil in the wok, swirling it around until it is really hot. Add the spring onions (scallions) and stir-fry for a minute or so, then add the chicken and stir-fry for 3–4 minutes until well sealed and almost cooked.

5 Add the courgettes (zucchini) and bamboo shoots and continue to stir-fry for 1–2 minutes.

Chicken with Celery & Cashew Nuts

Yellow bean sauce, widely available bottled, gives this easy Chinese dish a really authentic taste. Pecan nuts can be used in place of the cashews.

Serves 4

3–4 skinless, boneless chicken breasts, weighing 625g/1¼ lb

2 tbsp sunflower or vegetable oil

125 g/4 oz/1 cup unsalted cashew nuts

4–6 spring onions (scallions), sliced thinly diagonally

5–6 celery sticks (stalks), thinly sliced diagonally

175 g/6 oz jar of stir-fry yellow bean sauce

salt and pepper

celery leaves, to garnish (optional)

boiled rice, to serve

1 Cut the chicken into thin slices across the grain.

2 Heat the oil in the wok, swirling it around until really hot. Add the cashew nuts and stir-fry until they begin to brown, then add the chicken and stir-fry until well sealed and almost cooked through.

3 Add the spring onions (scallions) and celery and continue to stir-fry for 2–3 minutes, stirring the ingredients well around the wok.

4 Add the yellow bean sauce, season lightly with salt and pepper and toss until the chicken and vegetables are thoroughly coated with the sauce and piping hot. Serve at once with plain boiled rice, garnished with celery leaves, if liked.

Pan-cooked Chicken with Artichokes

Artichokes are a familiar ingredient in Italian cookery.
In this dish, they are used as a delicate flavouring with chicken.

Serves 4
4 chicken breasts, part boned
2 tbsp olive oil
30 g/1 oz/2 tbsp butter
2 red onions, cut into wedges
2 tbsp lemon juice
150 ml/¼ pt/⅔ cup dry white wine
150 ml/¼ pt/⅔ cup chicken stock
2 tsp plain (all-purpose) flour
425 g/14 oz can of artichoke hearts, drained and halved
salt and pepper
chopped fresh parsley, to garnish

1 Season the chicken with salt and freshly ground black pepper. Heat the oil and 15 g/½ oz/1 tablespoon of the butter in a large frying pan (skillet). Add the chicken and fry gently for 4–5 minutes on each side until lightly golden. Remove from the pan using a perforated spoon.

2 Toss the onions in the lemon juice, and add to the frying pan (skillet). Fry gently, stirring, for 3–4 minutes until just beginning to soften.

3 Return the chicken to the pan. Pour in the wine and stock, bring to the boil, then cover and simmer gently for 30 minutes.

4 Remove the chicken from the pan, reserving the cooking juices. Keep warm. Bring the juices to the boil, and boil rapidly for 5 minutes.

5 Blend the remaining butter with the flour to form a paste. Reduce the pan juices to a simmer and add the paste to the frying pan (skillet), stirring until thickened.

6 Adjust the seasoning, stir in the artichokes and cook for a further 2 minutes. Pour over the chicken and garnish with parsley.

Poached Breast of Chicken with Whisky Sauce

After cooking with stock and vegetables, chicken breasts are served with a velvety sauce made from whisky and crème fraîche.

Serves 6
30 g/1 oz/2 tbsp butter
60 g/2 oz/^{1}/$_2$ cup shredded leeks
60 g/2 oz/^{1}/$_3$ cup diced carrot
60 g/2 oz/^{1}/$_4$ cup diced celery
4 shallots, sliced
600 ml/1 pint/2^1/$_2$ cups chicken stock
6 chicken breasts
50 ml/2 fl oz/^{1}/$_4$ cup whisky
200 ml/7 fl oz/1 scant cup crème fraîche
2 tbsp freshly grated horseradish
1 tsp honey, warmed
1 tsp chopped fresh parsley
salt and pepper
parsley, to garnish

6 Pour a little of the whisky sauce around the chicken and pour the remaining sauce into a sauceboat to serve.

7 Serve with a vegetable patty made from the leftover vegetables, mashed potato and fresh vegetables. Garnish with parsley.

1 Melt the butter in a large saucepan and add the leeks, carrot, celery and shallots. Cook for 3 minutes, add half the chicken stock and cook for about 8 minutes.

2 Add the remaining chicken stock, bring to the boil, add the chicken breasts and cook for 10 minutes.

3 Remove the chicken and thinly slice. Place on a large, hot serving dish and keep warm.

4 In another saucepan, heat the whisky until reduced by half. Strain the chicken stock through a fine sieve, add to the pan and reduce the liquid by half.

5 Add the crème fraîche, the horseradish and the honey. Heat gently and add the parsley and salt and pepper to taste.

Garlicky Chicken Cushions

Stuffed with creamy ricotta, spinach and garlic, then gently cooked in
a rich tomato sauce, this is a suitable dish to make ahead of time.

Serves 4
4 part-boned chicken breasts
125 g/4 oz/$\frac{1}{2}$ cup frozen spinach, defrosted
150 g/5 oz/$\frac{1}{2}$ cup ricotta cheese
2 garlic cloves, crushed
1 tbsp olive oil
1 onion, chopped
1 red (bell) pepper, sliced
425 g/14 oz can chopped tomatoes
6 tbsp wine or chicken stock
10 stuffed olives, sliced
salt and pepper
flat leaf parsley sprigs, to garnish

1 Make a slit between the skin and meat on one side of each chicken breast. Lift the skin to form a pocket, being careful to leave the skin attached to the other side.

2 Put the spinach into a sieve and press out the water with a spoon. Mix with the ricotta, half the garlic and seasoning.

3 Spoon the spinach mixture under the skin of each chicken breast then secure the edge of the skin with cocktail sticks.

4 Heat the oil in a frying pan, add the onion and fry for a minute, stirring. Add the remaining garlic and red (bell) pepper and cook for 2 minutes. Stir in the tomatoes, wine or stock, olives and seasoning. Set the sauce aside and chill the chicken if preparing in advance.

5 Bring the sauce to the boil, pour into a shallow ovenproof dish and arrange the chicken breasts on top in a single layer.

6 Cook, uncovered in a preheated oven, 200°C/400°F/Gas Mark 6, for 35 minutes until the chicken is golden and cooked through. Test by making a slit in one of the chicken breasts with a skewer to make sure the juices run clear. Spoon a little of the sauce over the chicken breasts then transfer to serving plates and garnish with parsley. Serve with pasta.

Mediterranean Chicken Parcels

This method of cooking makes the chicken aromatic and succulent.

Serves 6
1 tbsp olive oil
6 skinless chicken breast fillets
250 g/8 oz/2 cups mozzarella cheese
500 g/1 lb/3¹/₂ cups courgettes (zucchini), sliced
6 large tomatoes, sliced
1 small bunch fresh basil or oregano
pepper

1 Cut six pieces of foil each about 25cm/10in square. Brush the foil squares lightly with oil.

2 With a sharp knife, slash each chicken breast at intervals, then slice the cheese and place between the cuts in the chicken.

3 Divide the courgettes (zucchini) and tomatoes between the pieces of foil and sprinkle with black pepper. Tear or roughly chop the herbs and scatter over the vegetables.

4 Place the chicken on top of each pile of vegetables then wrap in the foil to enclose the chicken and vegetables, tucking in the ends.

5 Place on a baking sheet and bake in a preheated oven, 200°C/400°C/Gas Mark 6, for about 30 minutes. To serve, unwrap each foil parcel and serve with rice or pasta.

Steamed Chicken & Spring Vegetable Parcels

A healthy recipe with a delicate oriental flavour, ideal for tender young summer vegetables. You'll need large spinach leaves to wrap around the chicken, but make sure they are young leaves.

Serves 4
4 boneless, skinless British chicken breasts
1 tsp ground lemon grass
2 spring onions (scallions), chopped finely
250 g/8 oz/1 cup young carrots
250 g/8 oz/1³/₄ cups young courgettes (zucchini
2 sticks (stalks) celery
1 tsp light soy sauce
250 g/8 oz/³/₄ cup spinach leaves
2 tsp sesame oil
salt and pepper

1 With a sharp knife, make a slit through one side of each chicken breast, to open out a large pocket. Sprinkle the inside of the pocket with lemon grass, salt and pepper. Tuck the spring onions (scallions) into the chicken pockets.

2 Trim the carrots, courgettes and celery then cut into small matchsticks. Plunge them into a pan of boiling water for 1 minute, then drain and toss in the soy sauce.

3 Pack into the pockets in each chicken breast and fold over firmly to enclose. Reserve the remaining vegetables. Wash and dry the spinach leaves then wrap the chicken breasts firmly in the leaves to enclose completely. If the leaves are too firm to wrap the chicken easily, steam them for a few seconds until they are softened and flexible.

4 Place the wrapped chicken in a steamer and steam over rapidly boiling water for 20–25 minutes, depending on size.

5 Stir-fry any leftover vegetable sticks and spinach for 1–2 minutes in the sesame oil and serve with the chicken.

Parma Wrapped Chicken Cushions

Stuffed with creamy ricotta, nutmeg and spinach, then wrapped with wafer thin
slices of Parma ham and gently cooked in white wine.

Serves 4
125 g/4 oz/¹⁄₂ cup frozen spinach, defrosted
125 g/4 oz/¹⁄₂ cup ricotta cheese
pinch grated nutmeg
4 skinless, boneless chicken breasts, each weighing 175 g/6 oz
4 Parma ham slices
30 g/1 oz/2 tbsp butter
1 tbsp olive oil
12 small onions or shallots
125 g/4 oz/1¹⁄₂ cups button mushrooms, sliced
1 tbsp plain flour
150 ml/¹⁄₄ pint/²⁄₃ cup dry white or red wine
300 ml/¹⁄₂ pint/1¹⁄₄ cups chicken stock
flat leaf parsley sprigs, to garnish

1 Put the spinach into a sieve and press out the water with a spoon. Mix with the ricotta and nutmeg and season with salt and pepper.

2 Slit each chicken breast through the side and enlarge each cut to form a pocket. Fill with the spinach mixture, reshape the chicken breasts, wrap each in a slice of ham and secure with cocktail sticks. Cover and chill.

3 Heat the butter and oil in a frying pan and brown the chicken breasts for 2 minutes on each side. Transfer the chicken to a large, shallow ovenproof dish.

4 Fry the onions and mushrooms for 2–3 minutes until lightly browned.

Stir in the flour then gradually add the wine and stock. Bring to the boil, stirring. Season and spoon the mixture around the chicken.

5 Cook the chicken uncovered in a preheated oven, 200°C/400°F/Gas Mark 6, for 20 minutes. Turn the breasts over and cook for a further 10 minutes. Remove the cocktail sticks and serve with the sauce. Garnish with the parsley and serve with carrot purée and green beans, if wished.

Chicken Lady Jayne

If you prefer just use boneless chicken breasts in this recipe.
This dish has a surprising combination of coffee and brandy flavours.

Serves 4
500 g/1 lb chicken breasts or supremes
4 tbsp corn oil
8 shallots, sliced
rind and juice of 1 lemon
2 tsp Worcestershire sauce
4 tbsp chicken stock
1 tbsp chopped fresh parsley
3 tbsp coffee liqueur
3 tbsp brandy, warmed

1 Cut the chicken breasts into 4 even pieces, cover them with cling film (plastic wrap) and beat them flat with a wooden meat mallet or a rolling pin.

2 Heat the oil in a large frying pan and fry the chicken for 3 minutes on each side, add the shallots and cook for a further 3 minutes.

3 Sprinkle with lemon juice and lemon rind and add the Worcestershire sauce and chicken stock. Cook for 2 minutes, then sprinkle with the parsley. Finally, add the coffee liqueur and the brandy and flame the chicken by lighting the spirit with a taper or long match. Cook until the flame is extinguished and serve.

COOK'S TIP

A supreme is a chicken fillet that sometimes has part of the wing bone remaining. Chicken breasts can be used instead.

Chicken Risotto à La Milanese

This famous dish is known throughout the world, and it is perhaps the best known of all Italian risottos, although there are many variations.

Serves 4
125 g/4 oz/$\frac{1}{2}$ cup butter
900 g/1$\frac{3}{4}$ lb chicken meat, sliced thinly
1 large onion, chopped
500 g/1 lb/2$\frac{1}{2}$ cups risotto rice
600 ml/1 pint/2$\frac{1}{2}$ cups chicken stock
150 ml/1/2 pint/$\frac{2}{3}$ cup white wine
1 tsp crumbled saffron
salt and pepper
60 g/2 oz/$\frac{1}{2}$ cup grated Parmesan cheese, to serve

1 Melt 60 g/2 oz/4 tbsp of butter in a deep frying pan, and when hot add the chicken and onion and cook until golden brown.

2 Add the rice, stir well, and cook for 15 minutes.

3 Heat the stock until boiling and add to the rice. Add the white wine, saffron, salt and pepper and mix well. Simmer gently for 20 minutes, stirring occasionally.

4 Leave to stand for a few minutes and just before serving add a little more stock and simmer for a further 10 minutes. Serve, sprinkled with the cheese and the remaining butter.

COOK'S TIP

There are many types of risotto rice with short, round grains. Arborio is a typical Italian risotto rice that is found in most supermarkets.

Savoury Chicken Sausages

Served with a smooth creamy tomato sauce,
this makes an excellent light lunch with freshly baked cheese bread.

Serves 4–6

175 g/6 oz/3 cups fresh breadcrumbs
250 g/8 oz cooked chicken, minced (ground)
1 small leek, chopped finely
pinch each of mixed herbs and mustard powder
2 eggs, separated
4 tbsp milk
crisp breadcrumbs for coating
30 g/1 oz/2 tbsp beef dripping(s)
salt and pepper

1 In a large clean bowl, mix together the breadcrumbs, chicken, leek, herbs and mustard powder, and season with salt and pepper.

2 Add 1 whole egg and an egg yollk with a little milk to bind the mixture.

3 Divide the mixture into 6 or 8 and shape into thick or thin sausages.

4 Whisk the remaining egg white until frothy. Coat the sausages first in the egg white and then in the crisp breadcrumbs.

5 Heat the dripping(s) and fry the sausages for 6 minutes until golden brown. Serve the sausages with a little tomato sauce.

COOK'S VARIATION

If you want to lower saturated fat in this recipe, use a little oil for frying instead of the dripping(s).

Tom's Toad in the Hole

This unusual recipe uses chicken and Cumberland sausage, which is then made into individual bite-sized cakes.

Serves 4–6
125 g/4 oz/1 cup plain (all-purpose) flour
pinch of salt
1 egg, beaten
200 ml/7 fl oz/1 scant cup milk
75 ml/3 fl oz/¹⁄₃ cup water
250 g/8 oz chicken breasts
250 g/ 8 oz Cumberland sausage
2 tbsp beef dripping(s)

1 Mix the flour and salt in a bowl, make a well in the centre and add the beaten egg.

2 Add half the milk, and using a wooden spoon, work in the flour slowly.

3 Beat the mixture until it is smooth, then add the remaining milk and water.

4 Beat again until the mixture is smooth. Let the mixture stand for at least 1 hour. Add the dripping(s) to individual baking tins (pans) or to one large baking tin (pan).

5 Cut up the chicken and sausage so that you get a generous piece in each individual tin (pan) or several scattered around the large tin (pan).

6 Heat the tins in a preheated oven, 220°C/425°F/Gas Mark 7, for 5 minutes until very hot. Remove the tins from the oven and pour in the batter, leaving space for the mixture to expand.

7 Return to the oven to cook for 35 minutes, until risen and golden brown. Do not open the oven door for at least 30 minutes.

8 Serve while hot, with chicken or onion gravy, or alone.

COOK'S VARIATION

Use skinless, boneless chicken legs instead of chicken breast in the recipe. Cut up as directed. Instead of Cumberland sausage, use your favourite variety of sausage.

Devilled Chicken

Chicken is spiked with cayenne and paprika and finished off with a fruity sauce.

Serves 2–3
30 g/1 oz/$^1/_4$ cup plain (all-purpose) flour
1 tbsp cayenne pepper
1 tsp paprika
350 g/12 oz skinless, boneless chicken, diced
30 g/1 oz/2 tbsp butter
1 onion, chopped finely
450 ml/$^3/_4$ pint/1$^7/_8$ cups milk, warmed
4 tbsp apple purée
125 g/4 oz/$^3/_4$ cup green (white) grapes
150 ml/$^1/_4$ pint/$^2/_3$ cup soured cream.
sprinkle of paprika

1 Mix the flour, cayenne and paprika together and use to coat the chicken.

2 Shake off any excess flour. Melt the butter in a saucepan and gently fry the chicken with the onion for 4 minutes.

3 Stir in the flour and spice mixture and slowly blend in the milk, stirring until the sauce thickens.

4 Simmer until the sauce is smooth.

5 Add the apple purée and grapes and simmer gently for 20 minutes.

6 Transfer the chicken and devilled sauce to a serving dish and top with soured cream and a sprinkle of paprika.

Quick Chicken Bake

This recipe is a type of cottage pie and is just as versatile. Add vegetables and herbs of your choice, depending on what you have at hand.

Serves 4
500 g/1 lb minced (ground) chicken
1 large onion, chopped finely
2 carrots, diced finely
30 g/1 oz/2 tbsp plain (all-purpose) flour
1 tbsp tomato purée (paste)
300 ml/1½ pint/1¼ cups chicken stock
pinch of fresh thyme
900 g/1¾ lb potatoes, creamed with butter and milk and highly seasoned
90 g/3 oz/¾ cup grated Lancashire cheese
salt and pepper

1 Dry-fry the minced chicken, onion and carrots in a non-stick saucepan for 5 minutes.

2 Sprinkle the chicken with the flour and simmer for a further 2 minutes.

3 Gradually blend in the tomato purée and stock then simmer for 15 minutes. Season and add the thyme.

4 Transfer the chicken mixture to an oven proof casserole and allow to cool.

5 Top the chicken with the mashed potato and sprinkle with the cheese. Bake in a preheated oven, 200°C/400°F/Gas Mark 6, for 20 minutes, then serve with peas.

Chicken in Rum & Orange Cream Sauce

A rich, orange cream sauce that is simplicity itself. Its luxurious texture comes from crème fraîche, but you can use single (light) cream instead.

Serves 4
2 tbsp sunflower oil
8 small, skinless chicken drumsticks
3 shallots or spring onions, chopped finely
200 ml/7 floz/scant 1 cup orange juice
4 tbsp dark rum
250 g/8 oz/1 cup long grain rice
grated rind of 1/2 orange
200 ml/7 floz/scant 1 cup crème fraîche or single cream
salt and pepper
orange segments (optional) and parsley to garnish

1 Heat the oil in a large pan and fry the chicken and the onions over a moderate heat until browned.

2 Add the orange juice and rum, cover tightly and simmer for 15 minutes or until the chicken juices run clear, not pink, when pierced with a skewer.

3 Meanwhile, cook the rice in boiling, lightly salted water until just tender. Drain and stir in the orange rind.

4 Stir the crème fraîche into the chicken and bring to the boil.

5 Season. Serve the chicken with the orange rice, garnished with orange segments, if using, and parsley.

Speedy Peanut Pan-fry

A complete main course cooked within ten minutes. Thread egg noodles are the ideal accompaniment because they can be cooked quickly and easily while the stir-fry sizzles, but any type of pasta or rice can be served instead.

Serves 4
300 g/10 oz/2 cups courgettes (zucchini)
250 g/8 oz/1⅓ cups baby corn (corn-on-the-cob)
250 g/8 oz/3 cups thread egg noodles
2 tbsp corn oil
1 tbsp sesame oil
8 boneless chicken thighs or 4 breasts, sliced thinly
300 g/10 oz/3¾ cups button mushrooms
350 g/12 oz/1½ cups beansprouts
4 tbsp smooth peanut butter
2 tbsp soy sauce
2 tbsp lime or lemon juice
60 g/2 oz/½ cup roasted peanuts
salt and pepper
coriander (cilantro), to garnish

5 Drain the noodles. Scatter with the peanuts and serve with the noodles. Garnish with coriander (cilantro).

COOK'S TIP

Try serving this stir-fry with rice sticks. These are broad, pale, translucent ribbon noodles made from ground rice.

1 Trim and thinly slice the courgettes (zucchini) and corn (corn-on-the-cob).

2 Cook the noodles in lightly salted boiling water for 3–4 minutes Meanwhile, heat the oils in a large frying pan or wok and fry the chicken over a fairly high heat for 1 minute.

3 Add the courgettes (zucchini), corn and mushrooms and stir-fry for 5 minutes.

4 Add the beansprouts, peanut butter, soy sauce, lime juice and pepper, then cook for a further 2 minutes.

Italian Chicken Spirals

Steaming allows you to cook without fat, and these little foil parcels retain all the natural juices of the chicken while cooking conveniently over the pasta while it boils. Sun-dried tomatoes, preserved in oil, have a wonderful, rich flavour, but if you can't find them use fresh tomatoes.

Serves 4
4 skinless, boneless, chicken breasts
30 g/1 oz/1 cup fresh basil leaves
15 g/$^1/_2$ oz/2 tbsp hazelnuts
1 garlic clove, crushed
250 g/8 oz/2 cups wholemeal (whole wheat) pasta spirals
2 sun-dried tomatoes or fresh tomatoes
1 tbsp lemon juice
1 tbsp olive oil
1 tbsp capers
60 g/2 oz/$^1/_2$ cup black olives
salt and pepper
sprigs of basil, to garnish

1 Beat the chicken breasts with a rolling pin to flatten evenly.

2 Place the basil and hazelnuts in a food processor and process until finely chopped. Mix with the garlic, salt and pepper.

3 Spread the basil mixture over the chicken breasts and roll up from one short end to enclose the filling. Wrap the chicken roll tightly in foil so that they hold their shape, then seal the ends well.

4 Add the pasta to a large pan of lightly salted, boiling water. Place the chicken parcels in a steamer basket or colander set over the pan, cover tightly, and steam for 10 minutes. Meanwhile, dice the tomatoes.

5 Drain the pasta and return to the pan with the lemon juice, olive oil,

tomatoes, capers and olives. Heat until warmed through.

6 Pierce the chicken with a skewer to make sure that the juices run clear

and not pink, then slice the chicken and arrange over the pasta. Garnish with sprigs of basil and serve with a tomato salad.

Golden Glazed Chicken

A glossy glaze with sweet and fruity flavours coats chicken
breasts in this tasty recipe.

Serves 6
6 boneless chicken breasts
1 tsp turmeric
1 tbsp wholegrain (whole-grain) mustard
300 ml/$\frac{1}{2}$ pint/1$\frac{1}{4}$ cups orange juice
2 tbsp clear honey
2 tbsp sunflower oil
350 g/12 oz/1$\frac{1}{2}$ cups long grain rice
1 orange
3 tbsp chopped mint
salt and pepper
mint sprigs, to garnish

1 With a sharp knife, mark the surface of the chicken breasts in a diamond pattern. Mix together the turmeric, mustard, orange juice and honey and pour over the chicken. Chill until required.

2 Lift the chicken from the marinade and pat dry on paper towels.

3 Heat the oil in a wide pan, add the chicken and sauté until golden, turning once. Drain off any excess oil. Pour over the marinade, cover and simmer for 10–15 minutes until the chicken is tender.

4 Boil the rice in lightly salted water until tender and drain well. Finely grate the rind from the orange and stir into the rice with the mint.

5 Remove the peel and white pith from the orange and segment.

6 Serve the chicken with the orange and mint rice, garnished with orange segments and mint sprigs.

COOK'S VARIATION

To make a slightly sharper sauce, use small grapefruit instead of the oranges.

Harlequin Chicken

This colourful, simple dish will tempt the appetites of all the family – it is ideal for toddlers, who enjoy the fun shapes of the multi-coloured peppers.

Serves 4
10 skinless, boneless chicken thighs
1 medium onion
1 each medium red, green and yellow (bell) peppers
1 tbsp sunflower oil
425 g/14oz can chopped tomatoes
2 tbsp chopped fresh parsley
pepper

1 Cut the chicken thighs into bite-sized pieces.

2 Peel and thinly slice the onion. Halve and deseed the peppers and cut into small diamond shapes.

3 Heat the oil in a shallow pan then quickly fry the chicken and onion until golden.

4 Add the peppers, cook for 2–3 minutes, then stir in the tomatoes and parsley and season with pepper.

5 Cover tightly and simmer for about 15 minutes, until the chicken and vegetables are tender. Serve hot with wholemeal (whole wheat) bread and a green salad.

COOK'S TIP

If you are making this dish for small children, the chicken can be finely chopped or minced first.

Golden Chicken Risotto

If you prefer, ordinary long grain rice can be used instead of risotto rice, but it won't give you the traditional, deliciously creamy texture that is typical of Italian risottos.

Serves 4
2tbsp sunflower oil
15 g/^{1}/$_2$ oz/1 tbsp butter or margarine
1 medium leek, thinly sliced
1 large yellow (bell) pepper, diced
3 skinless, boneless chicken breasts, diced
350 g/12 oz round grain (arborio) rice
few strands saffron
1.5 litres/2^1/$_2$ pints/6^1/$_4$ cups chicken stock
200 g/7 oz can sweetcorn (corn-on-the-cob)
60 g/2 oz/^{1}/$_2$ cup toasted unsalted peanuts
60 g/2 oz/^{1}/$_2$ cup grated Parmesan cheese
salt and pepper

1 In a large pan, heat the oil and butter. Fry the leek and (bell) pepper for 1 minute then stir in the chicken and cook, stirring until golden brown.

2 Stir in the rice and cook for 2–3 minutes.

3 Add the saffron, stock, salt and pepper. Cover and cook over a low heat, stirring occasionally, for about 20 minutes, until the rice is tender and most of the liquid is absorbed. Add more stock if necessary.

4 Stir in the sweetcorn (corn-on-the-cob), peanuts and Parmesan cheese, then adjust the seasoning to taste.

5 Serve hot with a crisp green salad.

Elizabethan Chicken

Chicken is surprisingly delicious when combined
with fruits such as grapes or gooseberries.

Serves 4
15 g/¹/₂ oz/1 tbsp butter
1 tbsp sunflower oil
4 skinless. boneless chicken breasts
4 shallots, finely chopped
150 ml/¹/₂ pint/²/₃ cup chicken stock
1 tbsp cider vinegar
175 g/ 6 oz/1 cup halved seedless grapes
120 ml/4 floz/¹/₂ cup double (heavy) cream
1 tsp freshly grated nutmeg
cornflour (cornstarch), to thicken, (optional)
salt and pepper

1 Heat the butter and oil in a wide, flameproof casserole or pan and quickly fry the chicken breasts until golden brown, turning once. Remove and keep hot.

2 Add the shallots to the pan and fry gently until softened and lightly browned. Return the chicken breasts to the pan.

3 Add the stock and vinegar, bring to the boil then cover and simmer gently for 10–12 minutes, stirring.

4 Transfer the chicken to a serving dish. Add the grapes, cream and nutmeg. Heat through, season to taste and serve hot. Thicken with a little cornflour if desired.

Chicken, Corn & Mangetout Sauté

This quick and healthy dish is stir-fried, which means you need use only the minimum of fat. If you don't have a wok, use a wide frying pan instead.

Serves 4
4 skinless, boneless chicken breasts
250 g/8 oz/1⅓ cups baby sweetcorn (corn-on-the-cob)
250 g/8 oz mangetout (snow peas)
2 tbsp sunflower oil
1 tbsp sherry vinegar
1 tbsp honey
1 tbsp light soy sauce
1 tbsp sunflower seeds
pepper

1 Slice the chicken breasts into long, thin strips. Cut the corn cobs in half lengthways and top and tail the mangetout (snow peas).

2 Heat the oil in a wok or a wide frying pan and fry the chicken over a fairly high heat, stirring, for 1 minute.

3 Add the corn and mangetout (snow peas) and stir over a moderate heat for 5–8 minutes, until evenly cooked.

4 Mix together the sherry vinegar, honey and soy sauce and stir into the pan with the sunflower seeds. Season well with pepper. Cook, stirring, for 1 minute. Serve hot with rice or Chinese egg noodles.

COOK'S TIP

Rice vinegar or balsamic vinegar makes a good substitute for the sherry vinegar.

Chicken Strips & Dips

Very simple to make and easy to eat with fingers, this dish can be served warm for a light lunch or cold as part of a buffet. For a lower fat alternative, poach the strips of chicken in a small amount of boiling chicken stock for 6–8 minutes, or until thoroughly cooked.

Serves 2
2 boneless chicken breasts
15 g/½ oz/2 tbsp plain (all-purpose) flour
1 tbsp sunflower oil
PEANUT DIP
3 tbsp smooth or crunchy peanut butter
4 tbsp natural yoghurt
1 tsp grated orange rind
orange juice (optional)
TOMATO DIP
5 tbsp creamy fromage frais
1 medium tomato, finely chopped
2 tsp tomato purée (paste)
1 tsp chopped fresh chives

1 Slice the chicken into fairly thin strips and toss in the flour to coat.

2 Heat the oil in a non-stick pan and fry the chicken until golden and thoroughly cooked. Drain well on absorbent paper towels.

3 To make the peanut dip, mix together all the ingredients (if liked, add a little orange juice to thin the consistency).

4 Combine the ingredients for the tomato dip and mix well.

5 Serve the chicken strips with the dips and a selection of vegetable sticks for dipping.

Chicken with Two Pepper Sauce

This quick and simple dish is colourful and healthy. It would be perfect for
an impromptu lunch or supper dish.

Serves 4
2 tbsp olive oil
2 medium onions, chopped finely
2 garlic cloves, crushed
2 red (bell) peppers, chopped
good pinch cayenne pepper
2 tsp tomato purée (paste)
2 yellow (bell) peppers, chopped
pinch of dried basil
4 skinless, boneless chicken breasts
150 ml/$^1/_4$ pint/$^2/_3$ cup dry white wine
150 ml/$^1/_4$ pint/$^2/_3$ cup chicken stock
bouquet garni
salt and pepper
fresh herbs, to garnish

4 Put the chicken breasts into a frying
pan and add the wine and stock. Add
the bouquet garni and bring the liquid
to simmer. Cook the chicken for about
20 minutes until tender.

5 To serve, put a pool of each sauce
onto four serving plates, slice the
chicken breasts and arrange on the
plates. Garnish with fresh herbs.

1 Heat 1 tablespoon of oil in each of
two medium saucepans. Place half the
chopped onions, 1 of the garlic cloves,
the red (bell) peppers, the cayenne
pepper and the tomato purée in one
of the saucepans. Place the remaining
onion, garlic, yellow (bell) peppers
and basil in the other pan.

2 Cover each pan and cook over a
very low heat for 1 hour until the
(bell) peppers are very soft. If either
mixture becomes dry, add a little
water. Process then sieve the contents
of each pan separately.

3 Return to the pans and season with
salt and pepper. The two sauces can
be gently re-heated while the chicken
is cooking.

Pies, Pastries & Terrines

Chicken once again shows its versatility in a splendid array of pastries and pies. Many of the pies and terrines can be made ahead of time and served cold, making them a good choice for a buffet, picnic or packed lunch. A thin slice of a terrine or pie can be served as a starter or a light meal, while a hearty slice of a traditional pie, such as Raised Chicken Pie, served with pickles and salad, makes a

satisfying main course. Various pastries are used for the pies, a choux pastry topping adorns Chicken and Sweetcorn Puff, while Sesame Chicken Pies, Chicken Filo Parcels (Packages) and Stilton & Walnut Strudel are all made from sheets of filo pastry. A suet pastry is used to make Old Fashioned Chicken Pudding and for Chicken, Cheese & Tarragon Pie, the base is made from shortcrust pastry while the topping is a golden puff pastry.

Chicken & Sweetcorn Puff

This delicious choux puff is an impressive dish yet it's simple to make.
You can use the choux pastry as a topping for all kinds of filling.

Serves 4

30 g/1 oz/2 tbsp butter
or margarine

30 g/1 oz/¼ cup plain
(all-purpose) flour

300 ml/½ pint/1¼ cups
skimmed milk

250 g/8 oz/1 cup skinless, boneless
cooked chicken, shredded

125 g/4 oz/¾ cup can sweetcorn
(corn-on-the cob), drained

1 tbsp chopped fresh parsley

salt and pepper

CHOUX PASTRY

75 g/2½ oz/generous ½ cup
plain (all-purpose) flour

60 g/2 oz/¼ cup butter
or margarine

150 ml/¼ pint/⅔ cup water

2 eggs, beaten

salt

4 Add the chicken, sweetcorn and parsley to the sauce. Season to taste. Pour into a 1 litre/1¾ pint/4 cup shallow baking dish.

5 Spoon the choux pastry around the edge of the dish. Bake in a preheated oven, 220°C/425°F/Gas Mark 7, for 35–40 minutes until puffed up and golden brown. Serve at once.

1 To make the choux pastry, sift the flour and salt into a bowl. Put the butter or margarine and water into a pan, then heat gently until the butter has melted. Bring to the boil. Remove from the heat and add the flour all at once. Beat with a wooden spoon until the mixture leaves the sides of the pan clean. Leave to cool slightly.

2 Gradually beat in the eggs until the mixture is thick and very glossy.

3 To make the filling, put the butter or margarine, flour and milk into a saucepan. Heat, whisking constantly, until smooth and thickened.

Three Fillet Parcel (Package)

Fillets of chicken, lamb and pork are layered with sage leaves, wrapped in spinach leaves, covered with a layer of cottage cheese and enclosed in puff pastry. This is delicious served cold and cut into slices.

Serves 6
300–350 g/10–12 oz pork fillet or tenderloin
about 12 fresh sage leaves
250–300 g/8–10 oz lamb neck fillet
2 skinless, boneless chicken breast fillets, weighing 300 g/10 oz
2 tbsp oil
125 g/4 oz/$^1/_3$ cup large spinach leaves
350 g/12 oz puff pastry, thawed if frozen
250 g/8 oz/1 cup cottage cheese
pinch of ground allspice
pinch of garlic powder
beaten egg or milk to glaze
salt and pepper
TO GARNISH
sage leaves
cucumber slices

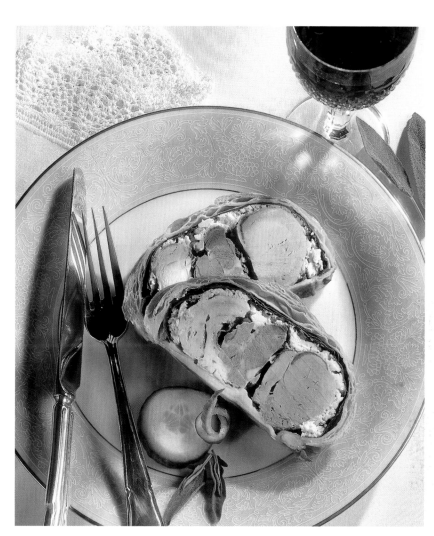

1 Layer the fillets beginning with the pork fillet. Cover with half the sage leaves, then add the lamb fillet, the rest of the sage leaves and finally the chicken fillets. Secure with string.

2 Heat the oil in a frying pan (skillet) and fry the layered fillets for about 15 minutes, turning until browned and partly cooked. Remove from the pan (skillet) and leave until cold.

3 Blanch the spinach leaves in boiling water for 2 minutes and drain well.

4 Roll out the pastry thinly into a rectangle large enough to enclose the layered fillets and allow for five narrow strips to be cut off the edge.

Cut off the strips, then lay the spinach in the centre of the pastry. Spread with the cottage cheese. Season and add the allspice and garlic powder.

5 Remove the string and place the fillets on top of the cheese and spinach. Wrap up in the pastry and seal the edges. Stand on a greased

baking sheet and glaze with egg. Lay strips of pastry over the roll and glaze.

6 Bake in a preheated oven, 200°C/400°F/Gas Mark 6, for 30 minutes. Reduce the temperature to 180°C/350°F/Gas Mark 4 and bake for 20 minutes. Cool, then chill. Slice and garnish with sage and cucumber.

Raised Chicken Pie

A filling of diced chicken leg meat, minced (ground) pork and bacon with pickled walnuts, mushrooms and herbs is enclosed in a hot-water pastry crust.

Serves 6
350 g/12 oz skinless, boneless chicken thighs
125 g/4 oz/$^1/_2$ cup lean raw pork, minced (ground)
125 g/4 oz/$^1/_2$ cup cooked ham, minced coarsely or chopped finely
1 small onion, very finely chopped
60 g/2 oz/$^2/_3$ cup button mushrooms, chopped roughly
1 tbsp chopped fresh parsley
good pinch of ground coriander seeds
6 pickled walnuts, well drained
beaten egg or milk to glaze
1 tsp powdered gelatine
150 ml/$^1/_4$ pint/$^2/_3$ cup chicken stock
salt and pepper

PASTRY
350 g/12 oz/3 cups plain (all-purpose) flour
1 tsp salt
90 g/3 oz/$^1/_3$ cup lard (shortening)
6 tbsp water
3 tbsp milk, for glazing

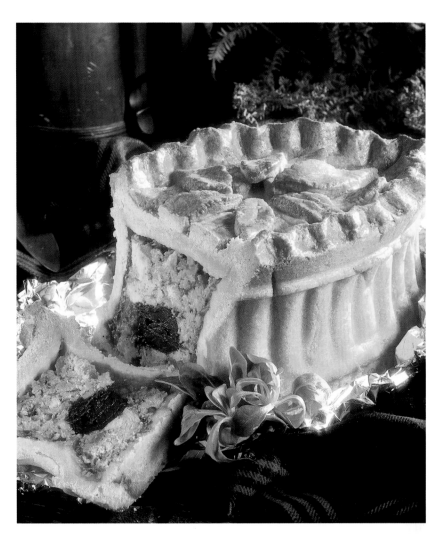

1 To make the filling, chop the chicken thighs and mix with the pork, ham, onion, mushrooms, parsley and ground coriander, and seasoning.

2 To make the pastry, sift the flour and salt into a bowl. Melt the lard in a saucepan with the water and milk and then bring to the boil. Pour onto the flour and mix to an even dough.

3 Roll out about three-quarters of the dough and use to line a lightly greased raised pie mould or a loaf tin.

4 Add half the chicken mixture to the mould, then a layer of walnuts and the remaining chicken. Roll out the reserved pastry, position over the chicken as a lid and cut a hole in the centre. Add pastry leaves and glaze.

5 Bake on a baking sheet in a preheated oven, 200°C/400°F/Gas

Mark 6, for 30 minutes. Reduce the temperature to 180°C/350°F/Gas Mark 4, glaze and bake for 1 hour. Remove from the oven. Cool for 10 minutes.

6 Dissolve the gelatine in the stock. Add as much stock as possible through the lid. Cool down then chill for 12 hours. Unmould before serving.

Chicken & Ham Pie

Made with yogurt shortcrust pastry, this pie has a really
moist filling and a melt-in-the-mouth crust.

Serves 6
60 g/2 oz/^{1}/4 cup butter
30 g/1 oz/^{1}/4 cup plain (all–purpose) flour
150 ml/^{1}/4 pint/^{2}/3 cup milk
150 ml/^{1}/4 pint/^{2}/3 cup natural yogurt
2 small leeks, sliced
250 g/8 oz skinless, boneless chicken breasts, diced
250g/8 oz/1^1/3 cups ham, diced
1 tsp soy sauce
black pepper
dill sprigs, to garnish

PASTRY

250 g/8 oz/2 cups plain (all–purpose) flour, plus extra for dusting
^{1}/2 tsp mustard powder
^{1}/4 tsp salt
175 g/6 oz/^{3}/4 cup butter, diced
about 3 tbsp natural yogurt
2 tbsp milk to glaze

1 To make the pastry, grease a loose-bottomed flan tin, 4 cm/1¾ inches deep. Sift together the flour, mustard powder and salt. Rub in the butter until the mixture resembles fine breadcrumbs. Stir in just enough yogurt to make a firm, non-sticky dough. Wrap in foil and chill.

2 Melt 30 g/1 oz/2 tablespoons of the butter in a pan. Blend in the flour. Add the milk and yogurt, stirring. Simmer, uncovered, for 5 minutes transfer the sauce to a bowl and cool.

3 Melt the remaining butter in a pan and fry the leeks for 2–3 minutes.

4 Pour the sauce over the leeks, add the chicken and ham, and cook for 3 minutes. Add the soy sauce, season with pepper, then leave to cool.

5 Roll out the pastry on a floured board. Use just over half to line the prepared tin. Add the filling. Roll out the remaining pastry and cover the pie. Trim the edges and press together. Brush the top with milk. Re-roll the trimmings and cut into decorative shapes. Arrange over the pie and brush with milk. Bake in a preheated, 200°C/400°F/Gas Mark 6, oven for 35 minutes, or until golden.

Sussex Huffed Pie

This modern version of a very old English classic uses chicken breasts wrapped in a light and crisp crust of vegetable suet crust pastry. The Bramley and walnut stuffing adds a delicious moist filling to each little parcel.

Serves 4
350 g/12 oz/3 cups self-raising (self-rising) flour, sifted
175 g/6 oz/1¼ cups vegetable suet
4 skinless, boneless chicken breasts
1 small Bramley apple, sliced thinly
30 g/1 oz/¼ cup chopped walnuts
2 tbsp chopped fresh sage
2 tbsp Worcestershire sauce
milk, to glaze
salt and pepper

1 Mix the flour and suet, and season. Stir in just enough cold water to bind to a firm, but not sticky dough. Divide into 4 and roll out each piece of dough to a 20 cm/8 inch round.

2 Cut a slit in the side of each chicken breast and pack with apple slices, walnuts and sage. Brush the pastry rounds all over with Worcestershire sauce.

3 Place a chicken breast on each pastry round.

4 Fold the pastry over and pinch the edges of the pastry together to seal. Lift onto a baking sheet and glaze with milk. Bake in a preheated oven, 200°C/400°F/Gas Mark 6, for 30–35 minutes until golden brown. Serve hot or cold.

Nell Gwynn's Chicken Pie

A traditional old English type of pie, subtly flavoured with oranges. If you prefer, it can be made with chicken off the bone instead of joints.

Serves 4

8 skinless chicken joints
(drumsticks and thighs)

200 g/7 oz/$\frac{1}{2}$ cup baby onions

1 large orange

120 ml/4 floz/$\frac{1}{2}$ cup
chicken stock

250 g/8 oz chilled or frozen
puff pastry, thawed

milk, for brushing

salt and pepper

FORCEMEAT

90 g/3 oz/1$\frac{1}{2}$ cups fresh wholemeal
(whole wheat) breadcrumbs

30 g/1 oz/2 tbsp finely chopped
cooked ham

2 tbsp chopped fresh parsley

finely grated rind 1 orange

1 tbsp sunflower oil

1 egg, beaten

1 Mix together all the ingredients for the forcemeat and season well with salt and pepper. Shape the mixture into 8 small balls.

2 Fry the chicken joints in a non-stick pan without fat, turning occasionally until golden brown. Drain and transfer to a 1.7 litre/3 pint/7$\frac{1}{2}$ cup pie dish.

3 Plunge the onions into a pan of boiling water and boil for 1 minute. Drain, rinse in cold water and remove the skins.

4 Cut away all the peel and white pith from the orange, then remove the segments. Add the onions, orange and forcemeat balls to the dish. Add the stock and season.

5 Roll out the pastry slightly larger than the pie dish and cut a 2.5 cm/ 1 inch wide strip from the edge. Brush the rim of the dish with milk and press on the strip of pastry to fit.

6 Cover the pie with the large piece of pastry. Press the edges to seal and brush with the milk. Place on a baking sheet in a preheated oven, 220°C/425°F/Gas Mark 7, for 10 minutes. Reduce the heat to 160°C/325°F/Gas Mark 3 and bake for a further hour. Serve hot with fresh green vegetables.

Chicken, Stilton & Walnut Strudel

A perfect choice for a cold buffet table, or serve hot with a red wine gravy for a dinner party main course. The combination of Stilton, mushrooms and walnuts helps enrich and moisten the filling without the need for a sauce to bind the ingredients. The strudel slices more easily when cold.

Serves 5–6
60 g/2 oz/4 tbsp butter
175 g/6 oz/2 cups oyster or flat mushrooms, sliced
2 shallots or spring onions, chopped finely
500 g/1 lb boneless, cooked chicken thighs, chopped finely
60 g/2 oz/$\frac{1}{2}$ cup walnut pieces
150 g/5 oz/1$\frac{1}{3}$ cups Stilton cheese, crumbled
3 tbsp fromage frais
1 tbsp chopped fresh thyme
7 sheets of filo pastry, each measuring 7$\frac{1}{2}$ x14 inches/19 x 35 cm
pepper

1 Melt 2 tablespoons butter and fry the mushrooms, shallots and chicken until the shallots are softened and any free liquid has evaporated.

2 Reserve a few walnuts for garnish and combine the rest with the mushrooms, shallots, chicken, Stilton cheese, fromage frais and thyme. Season with pepper.

3 Melt the remaining butter. Brush each sheet of pastry with butter then overlap the sheets to make one large square. Spoon the chicken mixture into the centre of the square.

4 Roll up carefully to enclose the filling, tucking in the ends.

5 Lift the roll carefully onto a greased baking sheet, brush with butter and scatter with the remaining walnuts.

Bake in a preheated oven, 190°C/375°F/Gas Mark 5, for 25–30 minutes until golden brown and firm. Serve hot or cold, with salad or vegetables.

COOK'S TIP

Fromage frais is a fresh curd cheese that varies in fat content. It is available both fat-free and with 8 percent fat.

Chicken Filo Parcels (Packages)

Perfect for a picnic or a packed lunch, these tasty chicken parcels (packages) can be packed into a rigid plastic container for carrying.

Serves 6
150 g/5 oz/$^1/_2$ cup frozen spinach, thawed
150 g/5 oz/$^1/_2$ cup feta cheese
6 skinless, boneless chicken thighs
12 sheets filo pastry, each measuring 7$^1/_2$ x14 inches/ 19 x 35 cm
2 tbsp sunflower oil
1 tbsp poppy seeds
pepper

1 Place the spinach in a sieve and press out excess moisture. Crumble the cheese then mix with the spinach and season with pepper.

2 Open out the chicken thighs on a board and place a spoonful of the spinach mixture on each. Fold over the chicken to enclose the filling.

3 Brush the sheets of filo pastry lightly with oil. Sandwich together in pairs, then place a piece of chicken on each. Roll up the pastry, tucking in the ends to enclose the filling.

4 Place on a baking sheet and brush with oil, then sprinkle with poppy seeds. Bake in a preheated oven, 200°C/400°F/Gas Mark 6, for 30–35 minutes, until golden brown and bubbling. Cool on a wire rack. Serve with a tomato salad.

Sesame Chicken Pies

This chicken pie is easy to make with ready-made filo pastry. Thigh meat is very economical and you can buy it ready diced, or just buy boneless thighs and chop them at home.

Serves 4

500g/1 lb diced chicken
thigh meat
1 tbsp cornflour
250 g/8 oz/1 cup crème fraîche
1 tbsp chopped fresh chives
1 medium onion, thinly sliced
120 ml/4 fl oz/½ cup
chicken stock
325 g/11 oz can sweetcorn
(corn-on-the-cob), drained
4 sheets filo pastry
2 tbsp olive oil
1 tsp sesame seeds
salt and pepper

1 Toss the chicken in the cornflour to coat evenly. Stir in the crème fraîche and chives and season.

2 Place the onion in a pan with the chicken stock and simmer over a moderate heat, stirring until the onion is softened and most of the stock is evaporated. Add to the chicken with the sweetcorn (corn-on-the-cob).

3 Transfer the mixture to a large pie dish or divide among four 300 ml/½ pint/1¼ cup ovenproof dishes. Place on a baking sheet.

4 Spread out the filo pastry and brush with oil.

5 Scrunch up the pastry to cover the filling of each pie. Sprinkle with sesame seeds.

6 Bake in a preheated oven, 190°C/375°F/Gas Mark 5, for 50–60 minutes until golden (individual pies will take 30–35 minutes). Serve hot with a green vegetable.

COOK'S TIP

Packaged filo pastry is available fresh and frozen. It can be stored for up to 1 year in the freezer.

Chicken wrapped in Puff Pastry with Lancashire Cheese & Mustard

This recipe is a variation on the classic Beef Wellington – and just as delicious.

Serves 6–8
500 g/1 lb chicken breast meat
45 g/1^1/$_2$ oz/3 tbsp butter
2 onions, chopped finely
125 g/4 oz/1^1/$_2$ cups button mushrooms or wild mushrooms
2 ready-rolled sheets puff pastry
2 tbsp English mustard
125 g/4 oz chicken liver pâté
125 g/4 oz/^{3}/$_4$ cup Lancashire cheese, crumbled
1 egg, lightly beaten
salt and pepper

1 With a sharp knife, trim the fat from the chicken and season well with salt and pepper.

2 Melt 2 tablespoons of butter in a large frying pan, add the chicken, and cook for about 4 minutes until sealed.

3 To the same pan, add the remaining butter and add the chopped onion and mushrooms. Cook until all the moisture has evaporated then allow to cool.

4 Roll out half of the pastry to a large rectangle and place on a greased baking sheet.

5 Spread the onion and mushroom mixture in the centre of the pastry and place the chicken on the mixture.

6 Top the chicken breasts with the mustard and liver pâté, then sprinkle them with a layer of the crumbled cheese.

7 Roll out the remaining pastry so it is slightly larger than the base.

8 Brush the edges of the pastry with egg then press together to seal.

9 Slash the top of the pastry with a sharp knife, then brush with egg.

10 Bake in the centre of a preheated oven, 200°C/400°F/Gas Mark 6, for 20 minutes, then lower the oven to 180°C/350°F/Gas Mark 4 for a further 20 minutes until golden brown.

Roast Chicken & Cranberry Pie

Cranberries are a good accompaniment to poultry
and make this pie very tasty, whether served hot or cold.

Serves 6
60 g/2 oz/4 tbsp butter
2 leeks, sliced finely
8 shallots, sliced
125 g/4 oz/1^{1}/$_{2}$ cups mushrooms, sliced
30 g/1 oz/^{1}/$_{4}$ cup plain (all-purpose) flour
300 ml/^{1}/$_{2}$ pint/1^{1}/$_{4}$ cups milk, warmed
150 ml/^{1}/$_{4}$ pint/^{2}/$_{3}$ cup double (heavy) cream
500 g/1 lb roast chicken meat, diced
150 g/5 oz/1 cup cranberry sauce
salt and pepper
175 g/6 oz shortcrust pastry for the base and 125 g/4 oz puff pastry for the top
1 egg, beaten, for glazing

1 Melt the butter in a large saucepan and gently fry the leeks, shallots and mushrooms for about 10 minutes, stirring occasionally.

2 Add the flour and cook for a further 2 minutes.

3 Gradually add the warm milk and cream, stirring continuously until the sauce becomes thick and creamy. Simmer for 2 minutes.

4 Add the chicken and cranberry sauce to the mixture.

5 Season well and allow the mixture to cool.

6 Roll out the shortcrust pastry for the base and use to line a greased ovenproof pie dish. Add the chicken mixture and top with the puff pastry.

Brush the top of the pie with the beaten egg. Bake in the centre of a preheated oven, 200°C/400°F/Gas Mark 6, for 30 minutes.

Chicken, Cheese & Tarragon Pie

The best way to prepare this type of pie is to make
a shortcrust base with a puff pastry topping.

Serves 6
60 g/2 oz/4 tbsp butter
2 carrots, diced finely
8 shallots, sliced
250 g/8 oz/3 cups button mushrooms, sliced
30 g/1 oz/¼ cup plain (all-purpose) flour
300 ml/½ pint/1¼ cups milk, warmed
150 ml/¼ pint/⅔ cup double (heavy) cream
500 g/1 lb chicken breast, cooked and diced
3 tbsp chopped fresh tarragon
60 g/ 2 oz/½ cup grated Cheddar cheese
salt and pepper
175 g/ 6 oz shortcrust pastry for the base and 125 g/4 oz puff pastry for the top
1 egg, for glazing

1 Melt the butter in a large saucepan
and gently fry the carrots, shallots
and button mushrooms for about 10
minutes, stirring occasionally.

2 Add the flour and cook for a further
2 minutes.

3 Gradually add the milk and cream,
stirring continuously until the sauce
becomes thick and creamy.

4 Simmer for 2 minutes.

5 Add the cooked chicken breast,
tarragon and cheese to the sauce.

6 Season well and allow the mixture
to cool.

7 Roll out the shortcrust pastry base
and use to line a greased, oval
ovenproof pie dish.

8 Add the chicken mixture and top
with puff pastry. Brush with the
beaten egg to glaze and bake in the

centre of a preheated oven,
200°C/400°F/Gas Mark 6 for 30
minutes or until the top is golden.

9 Serve with garlic creamed potatoes
and a green vegetable or salad.

Old Fashioned Chicken Pudding

This is a recipe from yesteryear made with suet pastry. Vegetable suet, which is made from hydrogenated vegetable oil is now an option if you don't want to use suet made from animal fat.

Serves 4
60 g/2 oz/4 tbsp butter
pinch of fines herbes
4 skinless chicken breasts, sliced
90 g/3 oz/1¼ cups button mushrooms
4 shallots, sliced
150 ml/¼ pint/⅔ cup fresh orange juice
1 sprig fresh thyme
4 tbsp brandy
150 ml/¼ pint/⅔ cup game or chicken stock, thickened
250 g/8 oz suet pastry
salt and pepper

1 Melt the butter in a large frying pan, add the fines herbes, sliced chicken breasts, button mushrooms and shallots and pan-fry them for 6 minutes. Remove the breasts from the pan.

2 Add the orange juice, thyme, brandy and seasoning to the pan and simmer for at least 20 minutes until the liquid is reduced by half.

3 Add the game stock, simmer and again reduce by half.

4 Line a 20 cm/8 inch basin with suet pastry.

5 Put the meat and game stock into the basin.

6 Cover the top of the basin with suet pastry and press the pastry layers gently together to seal.

7 Brush the top with melted butter.

8 Cover the basin with several layers of cooking foil.

9 Steam the pudding in a covered saucepan for 2 hours, topping up the pan with extra water as necessary. Serve with fresh vegetables.

Springtime Creamed Chicken & Vegetable Quiche

A quick-and-easy quiche that can be made even speedier
if you use ready-made pastry.

Serves 4–6
350 g/12 oz shortcrust pastry
30 g/1 oz/2 tbsp butter
6 spring onions (scallions)
125 g/4 oz/1 cup leeks, (white end) shredded
125 g/4 oz/1^1/$_2$ cups button mushrooms
125 g/4 oz/1 cup peas
175 g/6 oz/1^1/$_4$ cups grated Cheddar cheese
175 g/6 oz cooked chicken meat, sliced thinly
3 eggs
1 egg yolk
150 ml/^{1}/$_4$ pint/^{2}/$_3$ cup each milk and double (heavy) cream, mixed
salt and pepper

1 Roll out the pastry and use to line a 25 cm/10 inch fluted, loose-based flan tin (pan).

2 Melt the butter in a large frying pan and fry the spring onions (scallions), leeks, mushrooms and peas over a low heat for 6 minutes.

3 Remove from the heat, sprinkle the base of the quiche with half of the cheese then add the chicken and vegetables.

4 Finish with the remaining cheese.

5 Beat the eggs and egg yolk and the milk and cream mixture together and pour over the chicken and vegetables.

6 Bake in the centre of a preheated oven, 190°C/375°F/Gas Mark 5, for

35–45 minutes until the filling is set and golden brown.

COOK'S VARIATION

If you prefer, substitute single (light) cream for the milk and cream mixture.

Savoury Criss Cross

This is a very tasty picnic bake which can be served hot or cold.
Try serving it with home-made ginger beer.

Serves 6
350 g/12 oz ready-made shortcrust pastry
3 large hard-boiled (hard-cooked) eggs, sliced
8 slices lean, rindless streaky bacon, grilled (broiled) and chopped
250 g/8 oz cooked chicken, diced
250 g/8 oz/1^1/$_2$ cups sausage meat
1 egg beaten with 150 ml/^{1}/$_4$ pint/^{2}/$_3$ cup milk
salt and pepper

1 Roll out two-thirds of the pastry and use to line a buttered pie dish or a deep plate.

2 Arrange the eggs, bacon, chicken and sausage meat in the pastry case.

3 Pour over the egg and milk mixture.

4 Season well. Roll out the remaining pastry and cut into thin strips about 1 cm/^{1}/$_2$ inch wide, and lay them across the pie in a criss-cross pattern. Seal well all around the edges.

5 Bake in the centre of a preheated oven, 200°C/400°F/Gas Mark 6, for 10 minutes. Reduce the heat to 180°C/350°F/Gas Mark 4, and bake for a further 25 minutes.

COOK'S TIP

Use your favourite sausages in this recipe – simply remove and discard the sausage skins, then loosen the sausage meat with a fork.

Terrine of Chicken & Ham with Cranberry & Shallot Marmalade

This is a very impressive terrine that would be suitable for any special occasion. The cranberry and shallot marmalade is a perfect accompaniment.

Serves 6–8

500 g/1 lb chicken meat, roughly chopped
120 ml/4 fl oz/½ cup sherry
250 g/8 oz/1½ cups minced (ground) pork
1 small onion, chopped
3 eggs, beaten
500 g/1 lb lean cooked ham, diced
500 g/1 lb rindless streaky bacon

CRANBERRY & SHALLOT MARMALADE

2 onions, chopped
30 g/1 oz/2 tbsp butter
4 tbsp cranberries
1 tbsp brown sugar
8 shallots, chopped
salt and pepper

1 Remove any fat or sinews from the chicken meat, place it in a bowl with the sherry, and marinate for 3 hours. Add the pork, onion and the eggs. Season and mix thoroughly.

2 Mix the pieces of ham into the mixture.

3 Line a 1.2 litre/2 pint/5 cup ovenproof terrine dish with the bacon slices.

4 Add the chicken mixture, top with the remaining bacon, then cover with greased cooking foil.

5 Bake in the centre of a preheated oven, 180°C/350°F/Gas Mark 4, for 1½ hours. Remove the foil and allow to cool naturally, then chill for at least 4 hours before serving.

6 For the cranberry and shallot marmalade, fry the onions gently for 2 minutes in the butter. Season.

7 Add the cranberries, brown sugar and shallots and cook for 5 minutes.

Pour some cranberry and shallot marmalade onto individual plates and serve with a generous slice of the terrine. Garnish with orange slices and fresh bread.

Terrine of Chicken & Black Pudding

This is a recipe that you can make ahead of time
and store chilled until needed.

Serves 6–8
500 g/1 lb boneless chicken meat, roughly chopped
120 ml/4 fl oz/^{1}/$_2$ cup brandy
250 g/8 oz/1^1/$_2$ cups minced (ground) pork
^{1}/$_2$ onion, chopped
rind of 1 orange
3 eggs, beaten
500 g/1lb black pudding, diced
500 g/1 lb rindless streaky bacon
30 g/1 oz/2 tbsp butter
salt and pepper
orange slices and parsley, to garnish

before serving. Serve the terrine cut
into thick slices and garnish with
orange slices and parsley.

COOK'S TIP

Look for black pudding that
is low in fat.

1 Remove any fat or skin from the
chicken, place in a bowl with the
brandy and marinate for 3 hours.

2 Add the pork and the chopped
onion, the orange rind and the beaten
eggs. Season and mix the mixture
thoroughly.

3 Carefully add the black pudding to
the mixture, without breaking it up.

4 Line a 1.2 litre/2 pint/5 cup
ovenproof terrine dish with slices of
streaky bacon. Put in the chicken
mixture, cover with the remaining
bacon, then with greased cooking foil.

5 Stand the terrine in a baking tin
and add hot water to a level that is
half-way up the side of the terrine.

6 Bake in the centre of a preheated
oven, 180°C/350°F/Gas Mark 4, for 1½
hours. Remove the foil and allow to
cool, then chill for at least 4 hours

Potted Chicken & Cheese Terrine

Make this terrine at least two weeks before using it. This allows all the wonderful flavours of the cheeses, chicken, spices and sherry to blend together and mellow. Serve with warm oat cakes and a good port.

Serves 4
125 g/4 oz/1 cup Wensleydale cheese
125 g/4 oz/1 cup Lancashire cheese
350 g/12 oz cooked chicken fillet, shredded
125 g/4 oz/$^1/_2$ cup butter
1 tbsp English mustard
150 ml/$^1/_4$ pint/$^2/_3$ cup cream sherry
large pinch of mace
pinch of cayenne pepper
250 g/8 oz/1 cup butter

1 Crumble or grate the cheeses and place all the ingredients except the butter into a blender or food processor. Mix thoroughly, while slowly adding the sherry.

2 Place into individual ramekins and make the clarified butter.

3 Place the butter in a small saucepan and heat very gently, skimming off the foam as the butter heats.

4 Stand for 5 minutes then strain the butter through muslin (cheesecloth) into a bowl.

5 Pour the clarified butter over the mixture in the ramekins and leave to cool, then chill.

COOK'S TIP

Because the milk solids are not present in clarified butter, it keeps better than ordinary, unheated butter.

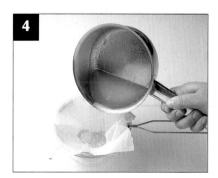

Chicken, Basil & Walnut Terrine

A terrine is a chunky pâté, which takes its name from the deep rectangular dish in which it is baked. If you don't have a terrine, a loaf tin can be used instead. This moist, basil-flavoured dish is ideal for summer meals and picnics, served with a simple salad.

Serves 6
250 g/8 oz/1¹/₃ cups streaky bacon
750 g/1¹/₂ lb skinless, boneless chicken thighs
280 g/9 oz/1 cup cream cheese or ricotta
15 g/¹/₂ oz/¹/₄ cup fresh basil leaves
1 tbsp sunflower oil
1 small onion, chopped finely
15 g/¹/₂ oz/1 tbsp butter
200 g/7 oz chicken livers, chopped
90 g/3 oz/1 cup mushrooms, chopped
45 g/1¹/₂ oz/¹/₂ cup walnuts, chopped
salt and pepper
sautéed mushrooms, to garnish

1 Stretch the bacon with the back of a knife and use to line a 1.75 litre/ 3 pint/7¹/₂ cup terrine dish or loaf tin.

2 Place one-third of the chicken, the cream cheese and the basil in a food processor and blend until almost smooth. Season well.

3 Heat the oil and fry the onion gently to soften. Finely chop the rest of the chicken and add to the pan, stirring until lightly coloured but not browned. Remove from the heat, stir in the cheese mixture and season the mixture well.

4 Spoon half the mixture into the terrine dish, smoothing the top until it is level.

5 Melt the butter and fry the chicken livers and mushrooms for 3–4 minutes, stirring until the chicken is lightly coloured.

6 Add the walnuts and spoon evenly over the chicken mixture. Top with the remaining chicken mixture.

7 Cover with a lid or foil and bake in a preheated oven, 180°C/350°F/Gas Mark 4, for 1–1¹/₄ hours, or until there is no trace of pink juices. Remove from the oven and place a weight on top. Leave to cool completely before turning out, or serve straight from the terrine dish. Garnish with sautéed mushrooms and serve in slices, with salad and French bread.

Chicken & Mushroom Terrine

This terrine is extremely quick to make if you use a food processor.
Sunflower seeds add a pleasing crunchy texture.

Serves 4
1tbsp oil
500 g/1 lb skinless, boneless chicken breasts, roughly chopped
250 g/8 oz/3 cups mushrooms
1 medium onion, quartered
1 garlic clove, crushed
30 g/1 oz/^{1}/$_2$ cup fresh brown breadcrumbs
3 tbsp chopped fresh parsley
3 tbsp chopped fresh sage
30 g/1 oz/2 tbsp sunflower seeds
salt and pepper

1 Brush a 1 litre/1^3/$_4$ pint/4 cup terrine dish or loaf tin with half of the oil.

2 Place the chicken, mushrooms and onion in a food processor and process until finely chopped.

3 Add the garlic, breadcrumbs, herbs and sunflower seeds, then season with salt and pepper.

4 Spoon the chicken mixture into the terrine and press down.

5 Brush with the remaining oil and loosely cover with foil. Bake in a preheated oven, 350°C/180°F/Gas Mark 4, for about 50 minutes, or until the juices run clear when the terrine is pierced with a skewer. Cool in the terrine then serve in thick slices with crusty bread.

Barbecues & Grills

There is nothing more delicious than the juicy flesh and charred skin of chicken that has been grilled over an open fire – after marinating in a flavourful mixture of oil and herbs or spices. Try an Asian-style mixture of yogurt and aromatic spices, or soy sauce, sesame oil and fresh ginger root, or a Cajun-inspired marinade of warm spices and garlic for Blackened Chicken with Guacamole. In this section, chicken comes in all shapes and sizes, it is minced to make Lemon & Mint Chicken Burgers, spatchcocked for Barbecued (Grilled) Chicken and cut into tiny, bite-sized pieces for Spicy Chicken Tikka. There are some unusual flavours and innovative tastes, including Skewered Chicken with Bramble Sauce, and Skewered Chicken Spirals, which are attractive whirls of chicken, bacon and basil. Baby chickens, flavoured with lemon and tarragon in this section, are perfect for grilling (broiling) or barbecuing.

Lemon & Mint Chicken Burgers

Use chicken leg meat for these delicious burgers – it has
much more flavour than breast meat.

Serves 4

750 g/1¹/₂ lb minced
chicken leg meat

4 tbsp chopped fresh mint

grated rind of 1 lemon

juice of 1 lemon

olive oil

90 g/3 oz/²/₃ cup pitted black olives,
chopped

1 round focaccia bread, either
plain or flavoured

lettuce leaf and lemon slices,
to garnish

salt

lemon pepper
(or black pepper)

1 In a large bowl, combine the chicken, mint, lemon rind, lemon juice, 1 tablespoon of olive oil, black olives, salt and lemon pepper. Leave to marinade for at least 2 hours.

2 Form the mixture into four patties, eliminating any air holes by pressing between your hands. Return to the refrigerator until ready to serve.

3 When ready to serve, cut the foccacia into four quarters, halve and brush each half with olive oil liberally, and toast under a grill (broiler) – do not use a toaster.

4 Fry the chicken patties in a little olive oil, for about 10 minutes, until cooked through. Remove the patties with a perforated spoon and drain on paper towels. Put each patty between two pieces of bread, and serve.

Barbecued (Grilled) Chicken

You need a bit of brute force to prepare the chicken, but once marinated it's an easy and tasty candidate for the barbecue (grill). Take great care not to touch your eyes or lips while preparing the chilli, and wash your hands thoroughly after handling.

Serves 4
1.5 kg/3 lb chicken
grated rind of 1 lemon
4 tbsp lemon juice
2 sprigs of rosemary
1 small red chilli, deseeded and chopped finely
150 ml/$\frac{1}{4}$ pint/$\frac{2}{3}$ cup olive oil

TO SERVE

minted new potatoes
green salad

1 Split the chicken down the breast bone and open it out.

2 Break the leg and wing joints to enable you to pound it flat. This ensures that it cooks evenly.

3 Mix the lemon rind and juice, rosemary sprigs, chilli and olive oil together in a small bowl. Place the chicken in a large dish and pour over the marinade, turning the chicken to coat it evenly. Cover the dish and leave the chicken to marinate for at least 2 hours or overnight.

4 Cook the chicken over a hot barbecue (grill) for about 30 minutes, turning it regularly until the skin is golden and crisp. To test if it is cooked, pierce one of the chicken thighs; if it is ready, the juices should run clear, not pink. Serve with minted new potatoes and a green salad.

Chicken in Spicy Yogurt

Make sure the barbecue (grill) is really hot before you start cooking.
The coals should be white and glow red when fanned. You could also cook
the chicken under a very hot preheated grill (broiler).

Serves 6
3 dried red chillies
2 tbsp coriander seed
2 tsp turmeric
2 tsp garam masala
4 garlic cloves, crushed
$^1/_2$ onion, chopped
2.5cm/1 inch piece fresh ginger root, grated
2 tbsp lime juice
1 tsp salt
120 ml/4 fl oz/$^1/_2$ cup natural yogurt
1 tbsp oil
2 kg/4 lb chicken, cut into 6 pieces, or 6 chicken portions
TO SERVE
chopped tomatoes
diced cucumber
sliced red onion
cucumber and yogurt

1 Grind together the chillies, coriander seed, turmeric, garam masala, garlic, onion, ginger, lime juice and salt with a pestle and mortar or grinder.

2 Gently heat a frying pan (skillet) and add the spice paste. Stir until fragrant, about 2 minutes. Turn into a shallow non-porous dish.

3 Add the yogurt to the spice paste and oil, and mix well to combine.

4 Remove the skin from the chicken portions and make three slashes in the flesh of each piece. Add the chicken to the dish and make sure

that the pieces are coated completely in the marinade. Cover and chill for at least 4 hours. Remove the dish from the refrigerator and leave covered at room temperature for 30 minutes before cooking.

5 Wrap the chicken pieces in foil, sealing well so the juices cannot

escape. Cook the chicken pieces over a very hot barbecue (grill) for about 15 minutes, turning once.

6 Remove the foil, with tongs, and brown the chicken on the barbecue (grill) for 5 minutes. Serve with the chopped tomatoes, diced cucumber, sliced red onion and yogurt mixture.

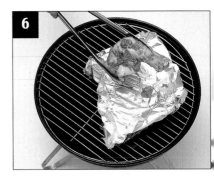

Chargrilled Chicken Salad

This is a quick dish to serve at a barbecue while your hungry guests are waiting for the main event. If the bread is bent in half, the chicken salad can be put in the middle and eaten as finger food – remember to provide napkins!

Serves 4
2 skinless, boneless chicken breasts
1 red onion
oil for brushing
1 avocado, peeled and pitted
1 tbsp lemon juice
120 ml/4 fl oz/$^{1}/_{2}$ cup mayonnaise
$^{1}/_{4}$ tsp chilli powder
$^{1}/_{2}$ tsp pepper
$^{1}/_{4}$ tsp salt
4 tomatoes, quartered
$^{1}/_{2}$ loaf sun-dried tomato-flavoured focaccia bread
green salad, to serve

1 Cut the chicken breasts into 1 cm/$^{1}/_{2}$ inch strips.

2 Cut the onion into eight pieces, held together at the root. Rinse under cold running water and then brush with oil.

3 Purée or mash the avocado and lemon juice together. Whisk in the mayonnaise. Add the chilli powder, pepper and salt.

4 Put the chicken and onion over a hot barbecue and grill for 3–4 minutes on each side.

5 Combine the chicken, onion, tomatoes and avocado mixture together.

6 Cut the bread in half twice, so that you have quarter-circle-shaped pieces,

then in half horizontally. Toast on the hot barbecue (grill) for about 2 minutes on each side.

7 Spoon the chicken mixture on top of the toasts and serve at once with a green salad.

Mediterranean Grilled Chicken

Chargrilling and barbecuing (grilling) are popular methods of cooking on the Mediterranean.
This recipe uses ingredients found in the Languedoc area of France,
where cooking over hot embers is a way of life.

Serves 4
4 tbsp natural yogurt
3 tbsp sun-dried tomato purée (paste)
1 tbsp olive oil
15 g/$\frac{1}{2}$ oz/$\frac{1}{4}$ cup fresh basil leaves, lightly crushed
2 garlic cloves, chopped roughly
4 chicken quarters
green salad, to serve

1 Combine the yogurt, tomato purée (paste), olive oil, basil leaves and garlic in a small bowl and mix well.

2 Put the marinade into a bowl large enough to hold the chicken quarters in a single layer. Add the chicken quarters, making sure they are thoroughly coated in the marinade.

3 Leave the chicken to marinate in the refrigerator for at least 2 hours or overnight. Remove and leave, covered, at room temperature for 30 minutes before cooking.

4 Place the chicken over a medium-hot barbecue (grill) and cook for 30–40 minutes, turning frequently.

5 Test for readiness by piercing the flesh at the thickest part – usually at the top of the drumstick. If the juices run clear, it is cooked through, but if the juices have blood in them, cook for 10 minutes longer.

6 Serve hot with a green salad. This is also delicious eaten cold.

Spicy Chicken Tikka

Arrange these tasty kebabs on a bed of finely shredded crisp lettuce, sliced onion and grated eating apple, drizzled with a little lemon or lime juice.

Serves 6
500 g/1 lb skinless, boneless chicken breasts
1¹/₂ tbsp Tikka paste (from a jar)
6 tbsp thick natural yogurt
1 tbsp lemon juice
¹/₂ onion, chopped finely
1¹/₂ tbsp chopped fresh chives or spring onion (scallion) tops
1¹/₂ tbsp finely chopped fresh ginger root
1–2 garlic cloves, crushed
1¹/₂ tbsp sesame seeds
2 tbsp vegetable oil
salt and pepper
wedges of lemon or lime, to garnish

1 Cut the chicken breasts into small bite-sized pieces, place in a shallow glass dish, and season with salt and pepper to taste.

2 In a small bowl, mix together the remaining ingredients, except the sesame seeds and oil, and pour over the chicken. Mix well until all the chicken pieces are coated, then cover and refrigerate for at least 1 hour, or for longer if possible.

3 Thread the chicken pieces on to six bamboo or metal skewers and sprinkle with the sesame seeds.

4 Place on a rack in a grill (broiler) pan and drizzle with the oil. Cook under a hot grill (broiler) for about 15 minutes or until cooked through and browned, turning frequently and brushing with more oil, if necessary. Serve hot, garnished with wedges of lemon or lime.

COOK'S TIP

Don't place the kebabs too near to the heat or the sesame seeds will burn before the chicken is cooked.

Tandoori Chicken

The tandoor is a traditional Indian oven shaped like a huge urn.
Charcoal is burnt slowly at the bottom until it becomes a mass of white-hot coals.

Serves 4
8 small chicken portions, skinned
3 dried red chillies
1 tsp salt
2 tsp coriander seeds
2 tbsp lime juice
2 garlic cloves, crushed
2.5 cm/1 inch piece fresh ginger root, grated
1 clove
2 tsp garam masala
2 tsp chilli powder
1/2 onion, chopped
300 ml/1/2 pint/1 1/4 cups natural yogurt
1 tbsp chopped fresh coriander (cilantro)
lemon slices, to garnish

CUCUMBER RAITA

250 g/8 oz/1 cup natural yogurt
2 tsp chopped fresh mint
175 g/6 oz cucumber, peeled, deseeded and cut into matchstick strips
salt

1 Make 2–3 slashes in the flesh of the chicken pieces and place in a non-metallic dish.

2 Crush the chillies, salt, coriander seeds, lime juice, garlic, ginger and clove. Stir in the garam masala and chilli powder. Transfer to a small pan and heat gently until aromatic.

3 Add the onion to the pan and fry. Stir in the yogurt and remove the pan from the heat.

4 Pour the yogurt mixture over the chicken. Cover and leave in the refrigerator for 4 hours or overnight.

5 Combine the raita ingredients in a small bowl. Cover and chill.

6 Arrange the chicken on a grill (broiler) tray and cook under a preheated very hot grill (broiler) or over a barbecue (grill) for 20–30 minutes, turning once, until the chicken juices run clear when the thickest parts of the portions are pierced with a sharp knife.

7 Sprinkle the chicken with chopped fresh coriander (cilantro). Serve hot or cold, garnished with the lemon slices and accompanied by cucumber raita.

Sesame Skewered Chicken with Ginger Baste

Chunks of chicken breast are marinated in a mixture of lime juice, garlic, sesame oil and fresh ginger to give them a spicy, aromatic flavour.

Serves 4
500 g/1 lb boneless chicken breasts
sprigs of fresh mint, to garnish

MARINADE

1 garlic clove, crushed
1 shallot, chopped very finely
2 tbsp sesame oil
1 tbsp fish sauce or light soy sauce
finely grated rind of 1 lime or 1/2 lemon
2 tbsp lime juice or lemon juice
1 tsp sesame seeds
2 tsp finely grated fresh ginger root
2 tsp chopped fresh mint
salt and pepper

1 To make the marinade, put the garlic, shallot, sesame oil, fish sauce or soy sauce, lime or lemon rind and juice, sesame seeds, ginger and chopped mint into a large non-metallic bowl. Season to taste with a little salt and pepper.

2 Remove the skin from the chicken breasts and cut the flesh into chunks. Add them to the marinade, stirring to coat them in the mixture. Cover and chill for at least 2 hours. Soak four wooden satay sticks in warm water for 30 minutes

3 Thread the chicken on to the wooden satay sticks. Place them on the rack of a grill (broiler) pan and baste with the marinade.

4 Place the kebabs under a preheated grill (broiler) for about 8–10 minutes. Turn them frequently, basting with the remaining marinade.

5 Serve at once, garnished with sprigs of fresh mint.

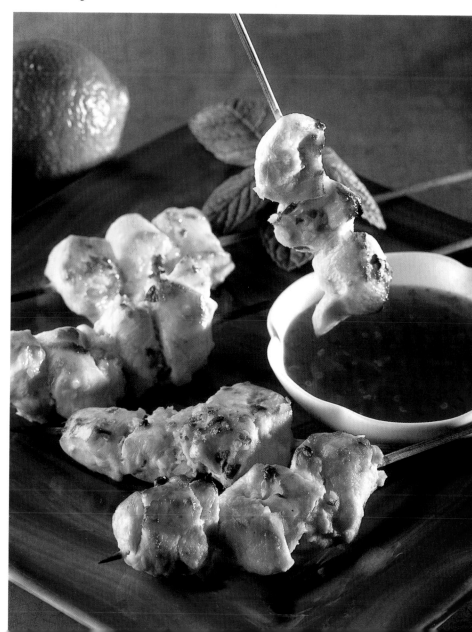

Crispy Chicken Drumsticks

Just the thing to put on the barbecue (grill) – chicken drumsticks, coated with a spicy, curry-like butter, then grilled until crispy and golden. Serve with a crisp green seasonal salad and rice.

Serves 6

12 chicken drumsticks

SPICED BUTTER

175 g/6 oz/³⁄₄ cup butter
2 garlic cloves, crushed
1 tsp grated fresh ginger root
2 tsp ground turmeric
4 tsp cayenne pepper
2 tbsp lime juice
3 tbsp mango chutney

TO SERVE

green salad
boiled rice

5 Serve hot or cold with a crisp green salad and rice.

COOK'S TIP

Add a few drops of chilli sauce to the spiced butter mixture to make the mixture hotter.

1 Prepare a barbecue (grill) with medium coals or preheat a grill (broiler) to moderate.

2 To make the spiced butter mixture, beat the butter with the garlic, ginger, turmeric, cayenne pepper, lime juice and chutney until it is blended well.

3 Using a sharp knife, slash each chicken drumsticks to the bone 3–4 times. Cook them on a barbecue (grill) for about 12–15 minutes or until almost cooked. Alternatively, grill (broil) the chicken for about 10–12 minutes until almost cooked, turning halfway through.

4 Spread the chicken legs liberally with the butter mixture and continue to cook for a further 5–6 minutes, turning and basting frequently with the butter until golden and crisp.

Blackened Chicken with Guacamole

This easy recipe is typical of French Cajun cooking which has its roots in earthy, strong flavours, and uses plenty of spice. The dish includes a typical Cajun spice mix.

Serves 4
4 skinless boneless chicken breasts
60 g/2 oz/¼ cup butter, melted

SPICE MIX
1 tsp salt
1 tbsp sweet paprika
1 tsp dried onion granules
1 tsp dried garlic granules
1 tsp dried thyme
1 tsp cayenne
½ tsp cracked black pepper
½ tsp dried oregano

GUACAMOLE
1 avocado
1 tbsp lemon juice
2 tbsp soured cream
½ red onion, chopped
1 garlic clove, halved

1 Put each chicken breast between two pieces of clingfilm (plastic wrap), and pound with a mallet or rolling pin until it is an even thickness. It should be about 1 cm/½ inch thick.

2 Brush each chicken breast all over with the melted butter. Set aside.

3 Combine the spice mix ingredients in a shallow bowl.

4 Coat the chicken breasts with the spice mix, ensuring that they are covered completely. Set aside.

5 To make the guacamole, mash the avocado thoroughly with the lemon

juice in a small bowl. Stir in the soured cream and red onion.

6 Wipe the garlic clove around the guacamole serving dish, pressing hard. Spoon in the guacamole.

7 Place the chicken breasts over the hottest part of a very hot barbecue and cook for 8–10 minutes, turning once.

8 Slice the breasts into thick pieces and serve immediately with the guacamole.

Jerk Chicken

This is a popular Caribbean dish. Rubbing pastes and 'rubs' into meat, poultry, fish or seafood is an old method of cooking introduced by the Arawak Indians that helps to tenderize the meat.

Serves 6
1.5 kg/3 lb chicken pieces
cherry tomatoes, to garnish
salad, to serve
MARINADE
6 spring onions (scallions)
2 fresh red chillies, preferably Scotch bonnet
2 tbsp dark soy sauce
2 tbsp lime juice
3 tsp ground allspice
$1/2$ tsp ground bay leaves
1 tsp ground cinnamon
2 garlic cloves, chopped
2 tsp brown sugar
1 tsp dried thyme
$1/2$ tsp salt

1 To make the marinade, chop the spring onions (scallions). Deseed and finely chop the chillies. Put the spring onions (scallions), chillies, soy sauce, lime juice, allspice, ground bay leaves, cinnamon, garlic, sugar, thyme and salt in a food processor or blender and blend until smooth. Alternatively, finely chop the spring onions (scallions) and chillies (being careful not to touch your eyes) add these to the remaining ingredients and, using a pestle and mortar, work to a chunky paste.

2 Place the chicken in a shallow dish and generously spoon over the marinade. Cover and leave in the refrigerator to marinate for 24 hours, turning each piece of chicken several times in the marinade.

3 Brush a grill (broiler) rack with oil and place the chicken on it. Grill (broil) under a preheated medium grill (broiler) for about 15–20 minutes on each side until the chicken juices run clear when the thickest part of each piece is pierced with a sharp knife.

4 Garnish with cherry tomatoes and serve with a salad.

Filipino Chicken

This recipe is from the Philippines. Tomato ketchup is a very popular ingredient in Asian dishes, as it has a tangy, sweet-sour flavour.

Serves 4
1 can lemonade or lime-and-lemonade
2 tbsp gin
4 tbsp tomato ketchup
2 tsp garlic salt
2 tsp Worcestershire sauce
4 chicken supremes or breast fillets
salt and pepper
TO SERVE
thread egg noodles
1 green chilli, chopped finely
2 spring onions (scallions), sliced

6 Serve the chicken with egg noodles, tossed with a little green chilli and spring onion (scallion).

COOK'S TIP

Wash your hands after handling chillies as their fiery seeds and flesh can cause painful burning.

1 Combine the lemonade or lime-and-lemonade, gin, tomato ketchup, garlic salt, Worcestershire sauce and seasoning in a large non-porous dish.

2 Put the chicken supremes into the dish. Cover the chicken completely with the marinade.

3 Leave to marinate in the refrigerator for 2 hours. Remove and leave, covered, at room temperature for 30 minutes.

4 Place the chicken over a medium barbecue (grill) and cook for 20 minutes. Turn the chicken once, halfway through the cooking time.

5 Remove from the barbecue (grill) and leave to rest for 3–4 minutes before serving.

Thai Chicken with Peanut Sauce

A favourite Thai dish, served with a spicy peanut sauce, that
can be made with chicken or beef.

Serves 4–6

4 skinless, boneless chicken breasts

MARINADE

1 small onion, finely chopped
1 garlic clove, crushed
2.5 cm/1 inch piece fresh
ginger root,
2 tbsp dark soy sauce
2 tsp chilli powder
1 tsp ground coriander seeds
2 tsp dark brown sugar
1 tbsp lemon or lime juice
1 tbsp vegetable oil

SPICY PEANUT SAUCE

300 ml/$^1/_2$ pint/1$^1/_4$ cups
coconut milk
4 tbsp/$^1/_3$ cup crunchy
peanut butter
1 tbsp fish sauce
1 tsp lemon or lime juice
salt and pepper

1 Trim any fat from the chicken
breasts then cut into thin strips,
about 7 cm/3 inches long.

2 To make the marinade, place all the
ingredients in a shallow dish and mix
well. Add the chicken strips and turn
in the marinade until well coated.
Cover and put in the refrigerator to
marinate for 2 hours or overnight.

3 Remove the chicken from the
marinade and thread the pieces,
concertina style, on bamboo or thin
wooden skewers.

4 Grill (broil) for 8–10 minutes,
turning and brushing occasionally
with the marinade, until cooked.

5 Meanwhile, to make the spicy
peanut sauce, mix the coconut milk

with the peanut butter, fish sauce and
lemon or lime juice in a pan. Bring to
the boil and cook for 3 minutes.
Season with salt and pepper to taste
and serve the sauce with the cooked
chicken satay.

Chicken Satay Kebabs

Small kebabs of satay chicken with cubes of cheese and cherry tomatoes
are served on crisp lettuce leaves.

Makes 8
1 tbsp sherry
1 tbsp light soy sauce
1 tbsp sesame oil
finely grated rind of ¹/₂ lemon
1 tbsp lemon or lime juice
2 tsp sesame seeds
500 g/1 lb skinless, boneless chicken breasts
90 g/3 oz/³/₄ cup Double Gloucester (brick) cheese or Gouda cheese
16 cherry tomatoes
crisp lettuce leaves, such as Little Gem
salt and pepper

PEANUT DIP

30 g/1 oz/¹/₃ cup desiccated (shredded) coconut
150 ml/¹/₄ pint/²/₃ cup boiling water
125 g/4 oz/¹/₂ cup crunchy peanut butter
good pinch of chilli powder
1 tsp brown sugar
1 tbsp light soy sauce
2 spring onions (scallions), trimmed and chopped

1 Combine the sherry, soy sauce, sesame oil, lemon rind, lemon or lime juice, sesame seeds, and salt and pepper in a bowl.

2 Cut the chicken into 2.5 cm/1 inch cubes. Add to the marinade and mix well. Cover and chill for 3–6 hours.

3 To make the dip, put the coconut in a saucepan with the boiling water and bring back to the boil. Leave until cold.

4 Add the peanut butter, chilli powder, sugar and soy sauce and bring slowly to the boil. Simmer gently, stirring, for 2–3 minutes until thickened, then cool.

5 Soak eight wooden skewers in warm water for 30 minutes. When the mixture is cold, stir in the spring onions (scallions). Turn into a bowl.

6 Thread the chicken on to eight wooden skewers. Cook under a moderate grill (broiler) for about 5 minutes on each side until cooked through. Leave until cold.

7 Cut the cheese into 16 cubes and add a cube and a cherry tomato to each end of the skewers.

8 Serve on lettuce with the dip.

Sticky Chicken Wings

These need to be eaten with your fingers so serve
them at an informal supper.

Serves 4–6
1 small onion, finely chopped
2 garlic cloves, crushed
2 tbsp olive oil
450 ml/³/₄ pint/1⁷/₈ cups tomato passata
2 tsp dried thyme
1 tsp dried oregano
pinch fennel seeds
3 tbsp red wine vinegar
2 tbsp Dijon mustard
pinch ground cinnamon
2 tbsp brown sugar
1 tsp chilli flakes
2 tbsp black treacle
16 chicken wings
salt and pepper

1 Soften the onion and garlic in the oil for about 10 minutes.

2 Add the passata, dried herbs, fennel seeds, vinegar, mustard and cinnamon to the pan with the sugar, chilli flakes, treacle, and salt and pepper. Bring to the boil, then reduce the heat and simmer gently for 15 minutes or so, until slightly reduced.

3 Put the chicken wings in a large dish, and coat liberally with the sauce. Marinade for 3 hours or as long as possible, stirring often.

4 Transfer the wings to a clean baking sheet (cookie sheet), and roast in a preheated oven, 220°C/425°F/Gas Mark 7, for 10 minutes. Reduce the heat to 190°C/375°F/Gas Mark 5 and cook for 20 minutes, basting often.

5 Serve piping hot with celery sticks (stalks) and cherry tomatoes.

COOK'S VARIATION

Instead of black treacle, use either honey or maple syrup for a different flavour and lighter colour.

Crispy-Coated Baby Chickens

You could adapt this recipe using a whole chicken or chicken pieces,
serving them on a bed of moist and colourful vegetables.

Serves 6
4 tbsp vegetable oil
60 g/2 oz/¼ cup butter
6 small baby chickens (poussins), trussed
1 large onion, sliced
500 g/1 lb baby carrots
1 tbsp flour
150 ml/¼ pint/⅔ cup white wine
juice of 2 oranges
2 fennel bulbs, quartered
300 ml/½ pint/1¼ cups chicken stock
½ tsp salt
1 tbsp black peppercorns, lightly crushed
1 tsp cornflour (cornstarch)
150 ml/¼ pint/⅔ cup thick natural yogurt
salt and pepper

COATING

3 tbsp demerara (brown crystal) sugar
1 tbsp black peppercorns, lightly crushed
3 tbsp coarse sea salt
150 ml/¼ pint/⅔ cup thick natural yogurt

1 Heat the oil in a large frying pan and add the butter. When bubbling, add the baby chickens in batches until golden. Remove and keep warm.

2 Add the onion to the pan and fry until translucent. Add the carrots, stir, then sprinkle with the flour and blend well. Add the wine and orange juice while stirring. Add the fennel, stock, salt and peppercorns. Bring to the boil then pour into a roasting tin.

3 Arrange the baby chickens in the roasting tin (pan), cover with foil and cook in the oven for 40 minutes.

4 To make the coating, stir together the sugar, peppercorns, salt and yogurt to make a thick paste.

5 Preheat the grill (broiler) to high. Remove the baby chickens from the roasting tin (pan) and place them on a rack. Spread the paste evenly over the baby chickens then grill (broil) for 3–4 minutes, until the coating is crisp.

6 Arrange the drained vegetables on a warm serving dish. Place the roasting tin (pan) over medium heat and bring the sauce to the boil. Stir the cornflour (cornstarch) into the yogurt then blend into the sauce. Taste for seasoning. Place the baby chickens in the centre of the dish, spoon a little sauce over the vegetables, and serve the rest separately.

Grilled (Broiled) Chicken Salad

Grilling (broiling) is a quick, healthy cooking method, ideal for sealing in the juices and flavour of chicken breasts, and a wonderful way to cook summer vegetables. Choose a good quality olive oil to enhance the fresh flavours to the full.

Serves 4
1 small aubergine (eggplant), sliced
2 garlic cloves, crushed
finely grated rind of $1/2$ lemon
1 tbsp chopped fresh mint
6 tbsp olive oil
4 boneless chicken breasts
2 medium courgettes (zucchini), sliced
1 medium red (bell) pepper, quartered
1 small bulb fennel, sliced thickly
1 large red onion, sliced thickly
1 small ciabatta loaf or 1 French baguette, sliced
extra olive oil
salt and pepper

1 Place the aubergine (eggplant) slices in a colander and sprinkle with salt. Leave over a bowl to drain for 30 minutes, then rinse and dry. Mix together the garlic, lemon rind, mint, and olive oil and season.

2 Slash the chicken breasts at intervals with a sharp knife. Spoon over about half of the oil mixture.

3 Combine the aubergines (eggplants) and the remaining vegetables, then toss in the remaining oil mixture. Marinate the chicken and vegetables for about 30 minutes.

4 Place the chicken breasts and vegetables on a preheated hot grill (broiler) or barbecue (grill), turning occasionally, until they are golden brown and tender, or cook on a ridged griddle pan on the hob. Brush the bread slices with olive oil and grill until golden.

5 Drizzle a little olive oil over the chicken and grilled vegetables and serve hot or cold with the crusty bread toasts and a salad.

Mustardy Barbecue Drummers

Great for barbecues (grills), or for simple summer lunches and picnics,
this is an easy and tasty recipe for chicken drumsticks.

Serves 4
10 slices smoked streaky bacon
1 garlic clove, peeled and crushed
3 tbsp wholegrain mustard
4 tbsp fresh brown breadcrumbs
8 chicken drumsticks
1 tbsp sunflower oil

1 Chop and fry two of the bacon slices without fat for 3–4 minutes, stirring. Remove from the heat and stir in the garlic, 2 tablespoons of mustard and the breadcrumbs.

2 Carefully loosen the skin from each drumstick. Spoon a little of the mustard stuffing under each, smoothing over firmly.

3 Wrap a bacon rasher around each drumstick, and secure with cocktail sticks (toothpicks).

4 Mix together the remaining mustard and the oil, brush over the chicken and cook on a preheated moderately hot barbecue or grill (broiler) for about 25 minutes, until there is no trace of pink in the chicken juices when pierced with a skewer. Serve hot or cold.

COOK'S TIP

Don't cook the chicken over the hottest part of the barbecue (grill) or the outside may be charred before the centre is cooked.

Skewered Spicy Tomato Chicken

These low-fat, spicy skewers are cooked in a matter of minutes – and they can be assembled ahead of time and stored in the fridge until you need them.

Serves 4

500 g/1 lb skinless, boneless
chicken breasts

3 tbsp tomato purée (paste)

2 tbsp clear honey

2 tbsp Worcestershire sauce

1 tbsp chopped fresh rosemary

250 g/8 oz cherry tomatoes

sprigs of rosemary,
to garnish

1 Cut the chicken into 2.5 cm/1 inch chunks and place in a bowl.

2 Mix together the tomato purée (paste), honey, Worcestershire sauce and rosemary. Add to the chicken, stirring to coat evenly.

3 Alternating the chicken pieces and tomatoes, thread them onto eight wooden skewers.

4 Spoon over any remaining glaze. Cook under a preheated hot grill (broiler) for 8–10 minutes, turning occasionally, until the chicken is thoroughly cooked. Serve on a bed of couscous or rice and garnish with sprigs of rosemary.

COOK'S TIP

Couscous is made from semolina that has been made into separate grains. It usually just needs moistening or steaming before serving.

Barbecued Chicken Quarters with Warm Aioli

Chicken quarters are barbecued (grilled) then served with a strongly flavoured garlic mayonnaise, which originated in Provence, France.

Serves 4

4 chicken quarters
2 tbsp oil
2 tbsp lemon juice
2 tsp dried thyme
salt and pepper

AIOLI

5 garlic cloves, crushed
2 egg yolks
120 ml/4 fl oz/$\frac{1}{2}$ cup each
olive oil and sunflower oil
2 tsp lemon juice
2 tbsp boiling water

marinade and turn the portions so that they cook evenly. Remove and arrange on a serving plate.

5 Beat the water into the aioli and turn into a warmed serving bowl. Serve with the chicken.

COOK'S TIP

To make a quick aioli, add the garlic to 300 ml/$\frac{1}{2}$ pint/1$\frac{1}{4}$ cups good quality mayonnaise then place in a bowl over a pan of warm water and beat together. Just before serving add 1–2 tablespoons of hot water.

1 Using a skewer, prick the chicken quarters in several places then place them in a shallow dish.

2 Mix the oil, lemon juice, thyme and seasoning together, then pour over the chicken. Turn the chicken quarters to ensure they are well coated with the marinade. Set aside for 2 hours.

3 To make the aioli, put the garlic in a bowl with a pinch of salt and beat together to make a paste. Add the egg yolks and beat well. Gradually add the oils, drop by drop, beating vigorously, until the mayonnaise becomes creamy and smooth. Add the oils in a thin steady trickle and continue beating until the aioli is thick. Stir in the lemon juice and season with pepper. Set aside in a warm place.

4 Place the chicken on a preheated barbecue (grill) and cook for about 25–30 minutes. Brush with the

Skewered Chicken with Bramble Sauce

This autumnal recipe can be made with fresh-picked wild blackberries from the hedgerow if you're lucky enough to have a good supply.

Serves 4
4 chicken breasts or 8 thighs
4 tbsp dry white wine or cider
2 tbsp chopped fresh rosemary
pepper
rosemary sprigs
and blackberries, to garnish

SAUCE
200 g/7 oz/scant 2 cups blackberries
1 tbsp cider vinegar
2 tbsp redcurrant jelly
1/4 tsp grated nutmeg

1 Cut the chicken into 2.5cm/1 inch pieces and place in a bowl. Sprinkle over the wine and rosemary, and season well with pepper. Cover and leave to marinate for at least an hour.

2 Drain the marinade from the chicken and thread the meat onto 8 metal or wooden skewers.

3 Cook on a preheated moderately hot grill (broiler) for 8–10 minutes, turning occasionally, until golden and evenly cooked.

4 Meanwhile, to make the sauce, place the marinade in a pan with the blackberries and simmer gently until soft. Press though a sieve.

5 Return to the pan with the cider vinegar and redcurrant jelly and bring to the boil. Boil uncovered until the sauce is reduced by about one-third.

6 Spoon a little bramble sauce onto each plate and place a chicken skewer on top. Sprinkle with nutmeg and serve hot. Garnish with rosemary and blackberries.

COOK'S TIP

If you use canned fruit, omit the redcurrant jelly.

Chicken Cajun-Style

These spicy chicken wings are good served with a chilli salsa and salad.

Serves 4
16 chicken wings
4 tsp paprika
2 tsp ground coriander
1 tsp celery salt
1 tsp ground cumin
$1/2$ tsp cayenne
$1/2$ tsp salt
1 tbsp oil
2 tbsp red wine vinegar

1 Wash and dry the chicken wings and remove the wing tips.

2 Mix together the paprika, coriander, celery salt, cumin, cayenne, the salt, oil and vinegar.

3 Rub this mixture over the wings and set aside, in the refrigerator, for a least 1 hour to allow the flavours to permeate the chicken.

4 Cook the wings on a preheated barbecue (grill), occasionally brushing with oil, for about 15 minutes, turning often until cooked through.

COOK'S TIP

To save time, you can buy ready-made Cajun spice seasoning to rub over the chicken wings.

Chicken with Garden Herbs

Warm weather calls for lighter eating, and this chilled chicken dish in a subtle herb vinaigrette is ideal for a summer dinner party, or for a picnic. The chicken can be cooked several hours before you need it and stored in the fridge until required.

Serves 4
4 part-boned, skinless chicken breasts
6 tbsp olive oil
2 tbsp lemon juice
4 tbsp finely chopped summer herbs, such as parsley, chives and mint
1 ripe avocado
125 g/4 oz/$\frac{1}{2}$ cup low-fat fromage frais
pepper

1 Using a sharp knife, cut 3–4 deep slashes in the chicken breasts.

2 Place in a flameproof dish and brush lightly with a little of the olive oil. Cook the chicken on a preheated moderately hot grill (broiler) turning once until golden and the juices run clear when the chicken is pierced with a skewer.

3 Combine the remaining oil with the lemon juice and herbs and season with pepper. Spoon the oil over the chicken and leave to cool. Chill for at least 1 hour.

4 Mash the avocado or purée in a food processor with the fromage frais. Season with pepper to taste. Serve the chicken with the avocado sauce.

Ginger Chicken & Corn

Chicken wings and corn in a sticky ginger marinade are designed to be eaten with the fingers – there's no other way! The corn has a delicious nutty texture, and if fresh corn is unavailable, you can use thawed, frozen corn instead.

Serves 6
3 cobs fresh sweetcorn (corn-on-the-cob)
12 chicken wings
2.5cm/1in piece fresh ginger root
6 tbsp lemon juice
4 tsp sunflower oil
1 tbsp golden caster (superfine) sugar

1 Remove the husks and silks from the corn and cut each cob into 6 slices. Place in a large bowl with the chicken wings.

2 Peel and grate the ginger or chop finely. Mix together with the lemon juice, oil and sugar, then toss with the corn and chicken to coat.

3 Thread the corn and wings onto skewers, to make turning easier.

4 Cook under a preheated moderately hot grill (broiler) or barbecue (grill) for 15–20 minutes, basting with the gingery glaze and turning frequently until the corn is golden brown and tender and the chicken is cooked. Serve with jacket potatoes or salad.

COOK'S TIP

Cut off the wing tips before grilling (broiling) as they burn very easily. Or you can cover them with small pieces of foil.

Skewered Chicken Spirals

These unusual chicken kebabs have a wonderful Mediterranean flavour, and the bacon helps keep them moist during cooking. They are quite easy to assemble, and can be made earlier in the day and refrigerated until needed.

Serves 4
4 skinless, boneless chicken breasts
1 garlic clove, crushed
2 tbsp tomato purée (paste)
4 slices smoked back bacon
large handful fresh basil leaves
oil for brushing
salt and pepper

1 Spread out a piece of chicken between two sheets of cling film (plastic wrap) and beat firmly with a rolling pin to flatten the chicken to an even thickness. Repeat with the remaining chicken.

2 Mix the garlic and tomato purée and spread over the chicken. Lay a bacon slice over each, then scatter with the fresh basil. Season well with salt and pepper.

3 Roll up each piece of chicken firmly, then cut into thick slices.

4 Thread the slices onto four skewers, making sure the skewer holds the chicken in a spiral shape.

5 Brush lightly with oil and cook on a preheated hot barbecue (grill) or grill (broiler) for about 10 minutes, turning once. Serve hot with a green salad.

Grilled (Broiled) Baby Chickens with Lemon & Tarragon

Spatchcocked baby chickens are complemented by the delicate fragrance of lemon and tarragon and grilled (broiled).

Serves 2
2 baby chickens
4 sprigs fresh tarragon
1 tsp oil
30 g/1 oz/2 tbsp butter
rind of ¹/₂ lemon
1 tbsp lemon juice
1 garlic clove
salt and pepper
tarragon and orange slices, to garnish

1 Prepare the baby chickens, turn them breast-side down on a chopping board and cut them through the backbone. Crush each bird gently to break the bones so that they lie flat while cooking. Season each with salt.

2 Turn them over and insert a sprig of tarragon under the skin over each side of the breast.

3 Brush the chickens with oil and place under a preheated hot grill (broiler) about 13 cm/5 inches from the heat. Grill (broil) for about 15 minutes, turning half way, until lightly browned.

4 Meanwhile, to make the glaze, melt the butter in a small saucepan, add the lemon rind, lemon juice and garlic and season with salt and pepper.

5 Brush the baby chickens with the glaze, and cook for a further 15 minutes, turning them once and brushing regularly so that they stay moist. Garnish the chickens with

tarragon and orange slices and serve with new potatoes.

COOK'S TIP

Once the chickens are flattened, insert 2 metal skewers through them to keep them flat.

Tropical Chicken Skewers

Chicken is given a Caribbean flavour. The marinade keeps them
moist and succulent during cooking.

Serves 6
750 g/1¹/₂ lb boneless chicken breasts
2 tbsp medium sherry
3 mangoes
bay leaves
2 tbsp oil
2 tbsp coarsely shredded coconut
pepper

1 Cut the chicken into 2.5 cm/1 inch cubes and toss in the sherry, with a little pepper.

2 Cut the mangoes into 2.5 cm/1 inch cubes, discarding the stone and skin.

3 Thread the chicken, mango cubes and bay leaves alternately onto long skewers, then brush lightly with oil.

4 Grill (broil) the skewers on a preheated moderately hot grill (broiler) for 8–10 minutes, turning occasionally until golden. Sprinkle with the coconut and grill (broil) for a further 30 seconds. Serve the kebabs hot with a crisp green salad.

COOK'S TIP

Use mangoes that are ripe but still firm so that they hold together on the skewers during cooking. Another firm fruit that would be suitable is pineapple.

Spicy Sesame Chicken

This is a quick and easy recipe for the grill, perfect
for lunch or to eat outdoors on a picnic.

Serves 4
4 chicken quarters
150 g/5 oz/$\frac{1}{2}$ cup natural yogurt
finely grated rind and juice of 1 small lemon
2 tsp medium-hot curry paste
1 tbsp sesame seeds
lemon wedges, to serve

1 Remove the skin from the chicken
and slash the flesh at intervals with a
sharp knife.

2 Mix together the yogurt, lemon
rind, lemon juice and curry paste.

3 Spread the mixture over the
chicken and arrange on a foil-lined
grill (broiler) pan or baking sheet.

4 Place under a preheated moderately
hot grill (broiler) and grill for 12–15
minutes, turning once. Grill (broil)
until golden brown and thoroughly
cooked. Just before the end of the
cooking time, sprinkle the chicken
with the sesame seeds. Serve with a
salad, naan bread and lemon wedges.

COOK'S VARIATION

Poppy seeds, fennel seeds
or cumin seeds, or a mixture of all
three, can also be used to sprinkle
over the chicken.

Grilled Chicken with Pesto Toasts

This Italian-style dish is richly flavoured with pesto, which is a mixture of basil, olive oil, pine nuts and Parmesan cheese. Either red or green pesto can be used for this recipe. Passata is puréed, sieved (strained) tomatoes that you can buy in cans or jars.

Serves 4
8 part-boned chicken thighs
olive oil, for brushing
400 ml/14 fl oz/1²/₃ cups passata (strained tomatoes)
120 ml/4 fl oz/¹/₂ cup green or red pesto sauce
12 slices French bread
90 g/3 oz/1 cup freshly grated Parmesan cheese
60 g/2 oz/¹/₂ cup pine nuts or flaked almonds
basil sprig, to garnish

1 Arrange the chicken in a single layer in a wide flameproof dish and brush lightly with oil. Place under a preheated grill (broiler) for about 15 minutes, turning occasionally until golden brown.

2 Pierce with a skewer to ensure that the juices run clear.

3 Pour off any excess fat. Warm the passata and half the pesto sauce in a small pan and pour over the chicken. Grill (broil) for a few more minutes, turning until coated.

4 Meanwhile, spread the remaining pesto onto the slices of bread. Arrange the bread over the chicken and sprinkle with the Parmesan cheese. Scatter the pine nuts over the cheese. Grill (broil) for 2–3 minutes, until browned and bubbling. Serve hot garnished with a basil sprig.

Minty Lime Chicken

These tangy lime and honey-coated pieces have a matching sauce
or dip based on creamy natural yogurt. They could be served at a barbecue
or as a main course for a dinner party.

Serves 6
3 tbsp finely chopped mint
4 tbsp clear honey
4 tbsp lime juice
12 boneless chicken thighs
salt and pepper
SAUCE
150 g/5 oz/$^1\!/_2$ cup natural thick yogurt
1 tbsp finely chopped mint
2 tsp finely grated lime rind

1 Combine the mint, honey and lime juice in a bowl.

2 Use cocktail sticks to keep the chicken thighs in neat shapes and add the chicken to the marinade, turning to coat evenly.

3 Leave to marinate for at least 30 minutes. Cook the chicken on a preheated moderately hot barbecue (grill) or grill (broiler), turning frequently and basting with the marinade. The chicken is cooked if the juices run clear when the chicken is pierced with a skewer.

4 Meanwhile, mix together the sauce ingredients.

5 Remove the cocktail sticks and serve the chicken with a salad and the sauce for dipping or pouring.

Chicken Tikka & Mango Kebabs

Chicken tikka is one of the lower-fat dishes from India. Recipes vary and you can try your own combination of spices to suit your personal taste.

Serves 4
4 skinless, boneless, chicken breasts, cut into 2.5 cm/1 inch cubes
1 garlic clove, crushed
1 tsp grated fresh ginger root
1 fresh green chilli, deseeded and chopped finely
6 tbsp low-fat natural yogurt
1 tbsp tomato purée (paste)
1 tsp ground cumin seeds
1 tsp ground coriander seeds
1 tsp ground turmeric
1 large ripe mango
1 tbsp lime juice
salt and pepper
fresh coriander (cilantro) leaves to garnish

TO SERVE

boiled white rice
lime wedges
mixed salad
warmed naan bread

1 Place the chicken in a shallow dish.

2 Mix together the garlic, ginger, chilli, yogurt, tomato purée (paste), cumin, coriander, turmeric, and salt and pepper. Spoon over the chicken, mix well, cover and chill for 2 hours.

3 Slice down either side of the mango stone (pit) and cut the flesh into cubes. Toss in the lime juice, then cover and chill until required.

4 Thread the chicken and mango pieces on the skewers. Place them on a grill (broiler) rack and brush the

chicken with the yogurt marinade and any remaining lime juice.

5 Place under a preheated moderate grill (broiler) and cook for 6–7 minutes on each side, brushing once with the marinade, until the chicken juices run

clear when the cubes are pierced with a sharp knife.

6 Serve on a bed of rice on a warmed platter with fresh coriander (cilantro) leaves, lime wedges, a mixed salad and warmed naan bread.

Sweet & Sour Drumsticks

Chicken drumsticks are marinated to impart a tangy, sweet and
sour flavour and a shiny glaze

Serves 4
8 chicken drumsticks
4 tbsp red wine vinegar
2 tbsp tomato purée (paste)
2 tbsp soy sauce
2tbsp clear honey
1tbsp Worcestershire sauce
1 garlic clove
good pinch cayenne
salt and pepper

1 Skin the chicken if desired and
slash 2–3 times with a sharp knife.

2 Put the chicken drumsticks into a
non-metallic container.

3 Mix all the remaining ingredients
and pour over the chicken.

4 Leave to marinate in the
refrigerator for 1 hour. Cook the
drumsticks on a preheated barbecue
(grill) for about 20 minutes, brushing
with the marinade and turning during
cooking. Serve with a crisp salad.

COOK'S TIP

For a tangy flavour, add the juice of
1 lime to the marinade. While the
drumsticks are grilling, check
regularly to ensure that they are
not burning.

Hot & Spicy

Because chicken is popular throughout the world, there are countless spicy recipes from Asia, Mexico, south-east Asia, the Caribbean, Spain and Japan. Lime juice, coriander (cilantro), fish sauce and fresh ginger root add the authentic tastes of Thailand to Thai-style Chicken Fried Rice, while Bang-Bang Chicken is a popular Szechuan dish from China with a sauce made from peanuts and sesame seeds. From Mexico comes Enchilada Layers – tortillas stacked up with layers of tomato sauce and spicy chicken, and Chicken Fajitas – chicken spiked with hot chillies, served in tortillas, and topped with soured cream, red onion and limes. Add Margueritas and you have a tasty Mexican spread. Baby Chickens with Green Peppercorns is a creative modern dish that would be perfect for any special occasion. It is served with rice cooked in a tasty sauce of peppercorns, mustard and wine.

Bang-Bang Chicken

The cooked chicken meat is tenderized by being pounded with a rolling pin,
hence the name for this very popular Szechuan dish from China.

Serves 4
1 litre/1³/₄ pints/4 cups water
2 chicken quarters (breast half and leg)
1 cucumber, cut into matchstick shreds

SAUCE

2 tbsp light soy sauce
1 tsp sugar
1 tbsp finely chopped spring onion (scallions)
1 tsp red chilli oil
¹/₄ tsp pepper
1 tsp white sesame seeds
2 tbsp peanut butter, creamed with a little sesame oil

1 Bring the water to a rolling boil in a wok or a large saucepan. Add the chicken pieces, reduce the heat, cover and cook for 30–35 minutes.

2 Remove the chicken from the pan and immerse it in a bowl of cold water for at least 1 hour to cool it, ready for shredding.

3 Remove the chicken pieces and drain well. Pat dry with paper towels, then take the meat off the bone.

4 On a flat surface, pound the chicken with a rolling pin, then tear the meat into shreds with two forks. Mix with the shredded cucumber and arrange in a serving dish.

5 To serve, mix together all the sauce ingredients and pour over the chicken and cucumber.

Thai-Style Chicken Fried Rice

A few special ingredients give this rice dish an authentic Thai flavour.

Serves 4
250 g/8 oz/generous 1 cup white long-grain rice
4 tbsp vegetable oil
2 garlic cloves, chopped finely
6 shallots, sliced finely
1 red (bell) pepper, deseeded and diced
125 g/4 oz French (green) beans, cut into 2.5 cm/1 inch lengths
1 tbsp Thai red curry paste
350 g/12 oz cooked skinless, boneless chicken, chopped
¹/₂ tsp ground coriander seeds
1 tsp finely grated fresh ginger root
2 tbsp Thai fish sauce
finely grated rind of 1 lime
3 tbsp lime juice
1 tbsp chopped fresh coriander (cilantro)
salt and pepper

TO GARNISH

lime wedges
sprigs of fresh coriander (cilantro)

1 Cook the rice in plenty of boiling, lightly salted water for 12–15 minutes until tender. Drain, rinse in cold water and drain thoroughly.

2 Heat the oil in a large frying pan (skillet) or wok and add the garlic and shallots. Fry gently for 2–3 minutes until golden.

3 Add the (bell) pepper and French (green) beans and stir-fry for 2 minutes. Add the Thai curry paste and stir-fry for 1 minute.

4 Add the cooked rice to the pan, then the chicken, ground coriander, ginger, fish sauce, lime rind and juice, and fresh coriander (cilantro). Stir-fry over a medium-high heat for about 4–5 minutes, until the rice and chicken are thoroughly reheated. Season to taste.

5 Garnish with lime wedges and coriander (cilantro) before serving.

Chicken Fajitas

This spicy chicken filling, made with mixed peppers, chillies and mushrooms and strongly flavoured with lime, is served in folded tortillas and topped with soured cream.
Many other fillings can be used – the possibilities are endless.

Serves 4
2 red (bell) peppers
2 green (bell) peppers
2 tbsp olive oil
2 onions, chopped
3 garlic cloves, crushed
1 chilli, deseeded and chopped finely
2 skinless, boneless chicken breasts, about 350 g/12 oz
60 g/2 oz button mushrooms, sliced
2 tsp chopped fresh coriander (cilantro)
grated rind of $\frac{1}{2}$ lime
2 tbsp lime juice
4 wheat or corn tortillas
4–6 tbsp soured cream
salt and pepper

TO GARNISH

sliced red onion
chopped tomatoes
lime wedges

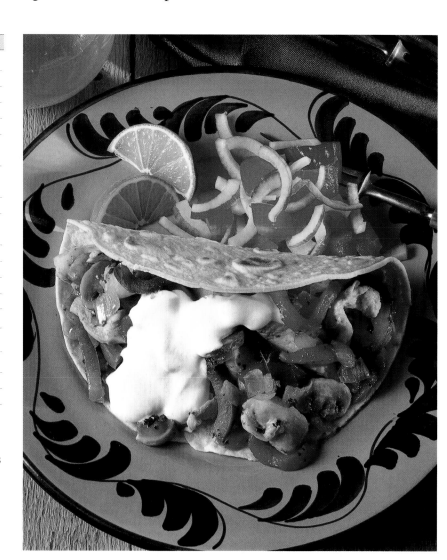

1 Halve the (bell) peppers, remove the seeds and place skin-side upwards under a preheated moderate grill (broiler) until well charred. Leave to cool slightly and then peel off the skin. Cut the flesh into thin slices.

2 Heat the oil in a pan, add the onions, garlic and chilli, and fry gently for a few minutes until the onion has softened.

3 Cut the chicken into narrow strips. Add to the vegetable mixture in the pan and fry for 4–5 minutes until almost cooked, stirring occasionally.

4 Add the peppers, mushrooms, coriander (cilantro), lime rind and juice, and continue to cook for 2–3 minutes. Season to taste.

5 Heat the tortillas, wrapped in foil, in a preheated oven, 180°C/350°F/ Gas Mark 4, for a few minutes. Bend them in half and divide the chicken mixture between them.

6 Top the chicken filling with a spoonful of soured cream. Serve garnished with red onion slices, chopped tomatoes and lime wedges.

Enchilada Layers

You can vary the filling for these layered Mexican tortillas by using beef,
fish or shellfish. If preferred, the tortillas can be rolled up once they are filled,
rather than baking them in layers.

Serves 4
500 g/1 lb boneless chicken breasts
2 tbsp olive oil
1 large onion, sliced thinly
3 garlic cloves, crushed
1 tsp ground cumin seeds
2 tbsp stock or water
1 tbsp chopped fresh coriander (cilantro)
6 wheat or corn tortillas
175 g/6 oz/$^3/_4$ cup feta cheese, coarsely grated
salt and pepper
sprigs of fresh coriander (cilantro), to garnish

TOMATO SAUCE

2 tbsp oil
1 onion, chopped very finely
3 garlic cloves, crushed
1 red chilli, chopped finely
425 g/14 oz can chopped tomatoes with herbs
200 g/7 oz can chopped tomatoes
3 tbsp tomato purée (paste)
2 tbsp lime juice
2 tsp caster (superfine) sugar
salt and pepper

1 Remove the skin from the chicken
and chop finely. Heat the oil and fry
the onion and garlic until softened.

2 Add the chicken and fry for 5
minutes. Add the cumin and stock.
Cook for 3 minutes until tender. Add
the coriander. Remove from the heat.

3 To make the tomato sauce, heat the
oil and fry the onion, garlic and chilli
gently until softened.

4 Add all the tomatoes, the tomato
purée, lime juice, sugar and seasoning.
Simmer gently for 10 minutes.

5 Cover a tortilla with a fifth of the
chicken mixture and 2 tablespoons of
the tomato sauce, then sprinkle with
grated cheese. Continue to layer in
this way, finishing with cheese.

6 Place the layered enchiladas in an
uncovered dish in a preheated oven,
190°C/375°F/Gas Mark 5, for 25
minutes, or until the top is lightly
browned. Serve in wedges, garnished
with a sprig of coriander (cilantro).

Chicken Burritos

A filling of chopped chicken, scrambled eggs, together with a spicy pumpkin seed, herb and yogurt mixture, and sliced tomatoes, is rolled into wheat or corn tortillas.

Serves 4
60 g/2 oz/¹/₂ cup pumpkin seeds
3–4 spring onions (scallions), trimmed and sliced
1 chilli, deseeded and chopped finely
4 tbsp chopped fresh flat leaf parsley
1 tbsp chopped fresh coriander (cilantro)
6 tbsp natural yogurt
4 wheat or corn tortillas
30 g/1 oz/2 tbsp butter
4 tbsp milk
1 garlic clove, crushed
6 eggs, beaten lightly
125 g/4 oz cooked skinless, boneless chicken, shredded
2 tomatoes, peeled and sliced
salt and pepper

TO GARNISH

shredded lettuce
sliced red onions
chopped tomatoes

1 Toast the pumpkin seeds lightly in a heavy-based frying pan (skillet) with no added fat. Chop finely, then put into a food processor with the spring onions (scallions) and chilli and blend or pound using a pestle and mortar.

2 Add the chopped parsley and coriander (cilantro), followed by the yogurt, and blend until well mixed. Season to taste with salt and pepper.

3 Wrap the tortillas in foil and warm for a few minutes in a preheated oven, 180°C/350°F/Gas Mark 4.

4 Melt the butter with the milk, garlic, and salt and pepper. Remove from the heat and stir in the eggs. Cook over a gentle heat, stirring, until just scrambled. Stir in the chicken.

5 Lay the tortillas flat and spoon some scrambled egg down the centre of each. Top the scrambled egg with the pumpkin seed mixture, then add the sliced tomatoes.

6 Roll up the tortillas and serve, garnished with the shredded lettuce, sliced red onions and tomatoes.

Chicken Paprika

Paprika, caraway seeds and soured cream give this dish an Eastern European flavour.
Paprika is a seasoning commonly used in Hungary.

Serves 4
60 g/2 oz/4 tbsp butter
4 chicken quarters
1 tbsp paprika
1 tbsp caraway seeds
1 onion, chopped finely
1 clove garlic, crushed
1 red (bell) pepper, finely chopped
125 g/4 oz/1 $\frac{1}{2}$ cups mushrooms, chopped finely
125 g/4 oz/$\frac{2}{3}$ cup pancetta, or smoked streaky bacon, diced
75 ml/3 fl oz/$\frac{1}{3}$ cup sherry
150 ml/$\frac{1}{4}$ pint/$\frac{2}{3}$ cup soured cream
1 tbsp cornflour (cornstarch)
salt and pepper

1 Heat the butter in a frying pan (skillet), add the chicken and brown well on all sides. Stir in the paprika and caraway seeds and season. Remove the chicken and set aside.

2 Add the onion and garlic to the pan and soften in the butter for about 10 minutes. Transfer the chicken and onions to a baking dish, cover and transfer to a preheated oven, 200°C/ 400°F/Gas Mark 6. Bake for 40 minutes, turning once or twice.

3 Remove the chicken and onions from the dish, reserving the cooking juices. Set aside to keep warm. Pour the cooking juices into a large frying pan (skillet) set over a moderate heat.

4 Stir in the pepper, mushroom and pancetta, and fry for 15 minutes.

5 Add the sherry, and simmer until reduced. Season to taste.

6 To finish the sauce, combine the soured cream and cornflour (cornstarch) and stir into the pan until the sauce is smooth and thick. Adjust the seasoning and serve the sauce with the chicken pieces.

Chicken, Coriander (Cilantro), Ginger & Lemon Stir-fry

The sweet and sour flavours in this recipe add a Chinese touch to this Indian stir-fry. The dish can be served cold in the summer with a spicy rice salad or a lettuce salad.

Serves 4

3 tbsp oil

750 g/1 1/2 lb skinless, boneless chicken breasts, cut in 5 cm/2 inch strips

3 garlic cloves, crushed

3.5 cm/1 1/2 inch piece fresh ginger root, cut into strips

1 tsp pomegranate seeds, crushed

1/2 tsp ground turmeric

1 tsp garam masala

2 fresh green chillies, sliced

1/2 tsp salt

4 tbsp lemon juice

grated rind of 1 lemon

6 tbsp chopped fresh coriander (cilantro)

120 ml/4 fl oz/1/2 cup chicken stock

naan bread, to serve

1 Heat the oil in a wok or large frying pan (skillet) and stir-fry the chicken until golden brown all over. Remove from the pan and set aside.

2 Add the garlic, ginger and pomegranate seeds to the pan and fry in the oil for 1 minute.

3 Stir in the turmeric, garam masala and chillies, and fry for 30 seconds.

4 Return the chicken to the pan and add the salt, lemon juice, lemon rind, coriander (cilantro) and stock. Stir the chicken to ensure it is thoroughly coated in the sauce.

5 Bring to the boil, then lower the heat and simmer for 10–15 minutes until the chicken juices run clear when the thickest part of the chicken is pierced with a sharp knife. Serve with naan bread.

COOK'S TIP

If you can't find pomegranate seeds, look for canned pomegranate juice instead and use 2 teaspoons in the recipe.

Chicken with Mushrooms

Try to find Chinese straw mushrooms for this dish. When cooked they are
brown and slippery and make a delicious addition to the chicken.

Serves 4

300–350 g/10–12 oz skinless,
boneless chicken

$^1/_2$ tsp sugar

1 tbsp light soy sauce

1 tsp rice wine or dry sherry

2 tsp cornflour (cornstarch)

4–6 dried Chinese
mushrooms, soaked in
warm water and drained

1 tbsp finely shredded fresh
ginger root

a few drops of sesame oil

salt and pepper

coriander (cilantro) leaves,
to garnish

1 Cut the chicken into small bite-sized pieces and place in a bowl. Add the sugar, soy sauce, wine and cornflour (cornstarch) and leave to marinate for 25–30 minutes.

2 Dry the mushrooms on paper towels. Slice into thin shreds, discarding any hard pieces of stem.

3 Place the chicken pieces on a heat-proof dish that will fit inside a bamboo steamer. Arrange the mushroom and ginger shreds on top of the chicken and sprinkle with sesame oil, and salt and pepper.

4 Place the dish on the rack inside a hot steamer or on a rack in a wok or large frying pan (skillet) filled with hot water. Steam over high heat for 20 minutes. Serve hot, garnished with coriander (cilantro) leaves.

Chicken with (Bell) Peppers

Sugar snap peas or celery can also be used in this spicy
Szechuan recipe to add extra crunchiness.

Serves 4

300 g/10 oz skinless, boneless
chicken breasts

1 tsp salt

$^1/_2$ egg white

2 tsp cornflour (cornstarch)
mixed to a paste
with 3 tsp cold water

1 green (bell) pepper

300 ml/$^1/_2$ pint/1$^1/_4$ cups
vegetable oil

1 spring onion (scallion),
shredded finely

a few strips of fresh ginger root,
shredded thinly

1–2 red chillies, deseeded
and shredded thinly

$^1/_2$ tsp sugar

1 tbsp rice wine or dry sherry

a few drops of sesame oil

1 Cut the chicken breast into strips,
then mix in a bowl with a pinch of
the salt, the egg white and cornflour
(cornstarch) paste.

2 Cut the (bell) pepper into thin
shreds the same size and length as
the chicken strips. Set aside.

3 Heat the oil in a preheated wok or
frying pan (skillet), and deep-fry the
chicken strips in batches for about 1
minute, or until the chicken becomes
golden brown and the strips are well
sealed. Remove the chicken strips
from the pan with a perforated spoon,
set aside and keep warm.

4 Pour off the excess oil, leaving
about 1 tablespoon in the wok. Add
the spring onion (scallion), ginger,
chillies and (bell) pepper. Stir-fry for
about 1 minute, then return the

chicken to the wok together with the
remaining salt, the sugar and the wine
or sherry. Stir-fry for another minute,
sprinkle with sesame oil and serve.

Quick Chinese Chicken with Noodles

Chicken and fresh vegetables are flavoured with ginger and Chinese five-spice powder in this quick and easy stir-fry. Vary the vegetables according to what is in season and make sure that they are as fresh as possible.

Serves 4
175 g/6 oz Chinese thread egg noodles
2 tbsp sesame or vegetable oil
30 g/1 oz/$\frac{1}{4}$ cup peanuts
1 bunch of spring onions (scallions), sliced
1 green (bell) pepper, cut into thin strips
1 large carrot, cut into matchstick strips
125 g/4 oz/1 cup cauliflower, broken into small florets
350 g/12 oz skinless, boneless chicken, cut into strips
250 g/8 oz/3 cups mushrooms, sliced
1 tsp finely grated fresh ginger root
1 tsp Chinese five-spice powder
1 tbsp chopped fresh coriander (cilantro)
1 tbsp light soy sauce
salt and pepper
fresh chives, to garnish

1 Put the noodles into a large bowl and cover with boiling water. Leave to soak for 6 minutes, or according to the instructions on the packet.

2 Meanwhile, heat the oil in a wok or large frying pan (skillet). Add the peanuts and stir-fry for about 1 minute until browned. Lift the peanuts out with a perforated spoon and drain on paper towels.

3 Add the spring onions (scallions), (bell) pepper, carrot, cauliflower and chicken strips to the pan. Stir-fry over a high heat for 4–5 minutes, until the chicken is cooked thoroughly. The vegetables should be still crisp, bright and colourful.

4 Drain the noodles thoroughly and add them to the wok. Add the mushrooms and stir-fry for 2 minutes.

Add the ginger, five-spice powder and coriander (cilantro) and stir-fry for another minute.

5 Season with the soy sauce, and salt and pepper. Sprinkle with the peanuts, garnish with chives and serve at once on warmed plates.

Lime & Coriander Chicken Fried Rice

Lime rind and lime juice are combined with chopped fresh coriander (cilantro)
to give this dish a lively Thai flavour.

Serves 4

250 g/8 oz/generous 1 cup
long-grain white rice

4 tbsp vegetable oil

2 garlic cloves, chopped finely

1 small green chilli, deseeded
and chopped finely

5 shallots, sliced finely

1 tbsp Thai green curry paste

1 yellow or green (bell) pepper,
chopped

2 celery sticks (stalks),
sliced finely

250 g/8 oz/1½ cups cooked skinless,
boneless chicken, chopped

2 tbsp light soy sauce

finely grated rind of 1 lime

2 tbsp lime juice

1 tbsp chopped fresh coriander
(cilantro)

30 g/1 oz/¼ cup unsalted peanuts,
toasted

TO GARNISH

sprigs of fresh coriander (cilantro)

finely sliced shallots

lime slices

1 Cook the rice in plenty of boiling, lightly salted water for about 12 minutes, until tender. Drain, rinse with cold water and drain thoroughly.

2 Heat the oil in a wok or large frying pan (skillet) and add the garlic. Fry gently for 2 minutes until golden. Add the chilli and shallots, and cook, stirring, for a further 3–4 minutes until slightly softened.

3 Add the Thai curry paste to the wok or frying pan (skillet) and fry for 1 minute, then add the yellow or green (bell) pepper and the celery. Stir-fry briskly for 2 minutes.

4 Add the cooked rice to the wok or frying pan (skillet) and add the chicken, soy sauce, lime rind and juice, and coriander (cilantro). Stir-fry over a medium-high heat for 4–5 minutes, until the rice and chicken are heated.

5 Serve sprinkled with peanuts. Garnish with sprigs of fresh coriander (cilantro), shallots and lime slices.

Baby Chickens with Peppercorns

Baby chickens are a good alternative to chicken. One bird serves two people and can be cooked whole. Sautéed cherry tomatoes are a colourful accompaniment.

Serves 4
2 baby chickens, halved, washed and dried
2 tbsp oil
30 g/1 oz/2 tbsp butter
1 onion, chopped
3 tbsp bottled green peppercorns
2 tbsp wholegrain mustard
120 ml/4 fl oz/½ cup white wine
200 g/7 oz/1⅓ cups basmati and wild rice
500 ml/16 fl oz/2 cups chicken stock
salt and pepper

1 Wash the chickens and pat dry. Heat the oil and butter, and cook the onion for 5 minutes until softened.

2 Season the chickens well with salt and pepper, and add to the pan. Brown all over then transfer to a baking sheet (cookie sheet).

3 Finish cooking the baby chickens in a preheated oven, 200°C/400°F/Gas Mark 6, for 30 minutes.

4 Meanwhile, stir the peppercorns, mustard and wine into the pan juices, bring to the boil and reduce by half.

5 Stir in the rice, and pour on the stock. Season well and bring to a simmer. Cook for 18–20 minutes. Adjust the seasoning, if necessary.

6 Serve the baby chickens piping hot on a bed of rice.

Spicy Chicken Tortillas

Serve these easy-to-prepare tortillas to friends or as a special family supper.
The chicken filling has a mild, mellow spicy heat and a fresh salad makes
a perfect accompaniment.

Serves 4
2 tbsp oil
8 skinless, boneless chicken thighs, sliced
1 onion, chopped
2 garlic cloves, chopped
1 tsp cumin seeds, roughly crushed
2 large dried chillies, sliced
425 g/14 oz can tomatoes
425 g/14 oz can red kidney beans, drained
150 ml/$\frac{1}{4}$ pint/$\frac{2}{3}$ cup chicken stock
2 tsp sugar
salt and pepper
lime wedges, to garnish

TO SERVE

1 large ripe avocado
1 lime
8 soft tortillas
250 ml/8 fl oz/1 cup thick yogurt

1 Heat the oil in a large frying pan or wok, add the chicken and fry for 3 minutes. Add the onion and fry for 5 minutes, stirring until browned. Add the garlic, cumin and chillies, with their seeds, and cook for about 1 minute.

2 Add the tomatoes, kidney beans, stock, sugar and salt and pepper. Bring to the boil, breaking up the tomatoes. Cover and simmer for 15 minutes. Remove the lid and cook for 5 minutes, stirring occasionally until the sauce has thickened.

3 Halve the avocado, discard the stone and scoop out the flesh onto a plate. Mash the avocado with a fork. Cut half of the lime into 8 thin wedges. Squeeze the juice from the remaining lime over the avocado.

4 Warm the tortillas as the pack directs. Put two tortillas on each serving plate, fill with the chicken mixture and top with spoonfuls of avocado and yogurt. Garnish the tortillas with lime wedges.

Kashmiri Chicken

This warming, rich and spicy dish is based on the traditional cooking style of Northern India, using chicken on the bone. If you prefer, use boneless chicken breasts instead of legs, and cut into large chunks for cooking.

Serves 4
4 skinless chicken drumsticks
4 skinless chicken thighs
150 ml/¼ pint/⅔ cup natural yogurt
4 tbsp Tikka curry paste
2 tbsp sunflower oil
1 medium onion, sliced thinly
1 garlic clove, crushed
1 tsp ground cumin
1 tsp finely chopped fresh ginger root
½ tsp chilli paste
4 tsp chicken stock
2 tbsp ground almonds
salt
fresh coriander (cilantro), to garnish

1 Slash the chicken fairly deeply at intervals with a sharp knife and place in a large bowl.

2 Mix together the yogurt and curry paste and stir into the chicken tossing to coat evenly. Cover and chill for at least 1 hour.

3 Heat the oil in a large pan and fry the onion and garlic for 4–5 minutes until softened but not browned.

4 Stir in the cumin, ginger and chilli paste and cook gently for 1 minute.

5 Add the chicken pieces and fry gently, turning occasionally, for about 10 minutes or until evenly browned. Stir in any remaining marinade with the stock and almonds. Cover the pan and simmer gently for a further 15 minutes or until the chicken is completely cooked and tender.

6 Season to taste with a little salt. Garnish the chicken with coriander (cilantro) and serve with pilau rice, pickles and poppadums.

Teppanyaki

This simple, Japanese style of cooking is ideal for thinly sliced breast of chicken. Mirin is a rich, sweet rice wine which you can buy in oriental shops, but if it is not available add one tablespoon of soft light brown sugar to the sauce instead.

Serves 4
4 boneless chicken breasts
1 red (bell) pepper
1 green (bell) pepper
4 spring onions (scallions)
8 baby corn cobs (corn-on-the-cob)
100g/4 oz/$^1/_2$ cup bean-sprouts
1 tbsp sesame or sunflower oil
4 tbsp soy sauce
4 tbsp mirin
1 tbsp grated fresh ginger root

1 Remove the skin from the chicken and slice at a slight angle, to a thickness of about 5 mm/¼ inch.

2 Deseed and thinly slice the (bell) peppers and trim and slice the spring onions (scallions) and corn cobs (corn-on-the-cob). Arrange the (bell) peppers, spring onions (scallions), corn and bean-sprouts on a plate with the sliced chicken.

3 Heat a large griddle or heavy frying pan then lightly brush with oil. Add the vegetables and chicken slices in small batches, allowing space between them so that they cook thoroughly.

4 Combine the soy sauce, mirin and ginger and serve as a dip with the chicken and vegetables.

Spanish Chicken with Prawns

This unusual dish, with its mixture of chicken and shellfish, is typically Spanish.
The basis of this recipe is sofrito: a slow-cooked mixture of onion and tomato in olive oil, with
garlic and peppers. Chorizo, a cooked, spicy Spanish sausage, is also used in this recipe.

Serves 4
4 chicken quarters
1 tbsp olive oil
1 red (bell) pepper
1 medium onion
2 garlic cloves, crushed
425 g/14 oz can chopped tomatoes
200 ml/7 fl oz/scant 1 cup dry white wine
4 tbsp chopped fresh oregano
125 g/4 oz/1 cup chorizo sausage
125 g/4 oz/1 cup peeled prawns (shrimp)
salt and pepper

1 Remove the skin from the chicken. Heat the oil in a wide, heavy pan and fry the chicken, turning occasionally until golden brown.

2 Deseed and slice the (bell) pepper and peel and slice the onion. Add to the pan and fry gently to soften.

3 Add the garlic with the tomatoes, wine and oregano. Season well, then bring to the boil, cover and simmer gently for 45 minutes or until the chicken is tender and the juices run clear when the chicken is pierced with a skewer.

4 Thinly slice the chorizo and add with the prawns (shrimp), then simmer for a further 5 minutes. Season to taste and serve with rice.

Regal Chicken with Cashew Nut Stuffing

Most of the flavourful stuffing is cooked separately from the chicken, only a small amount is added to the neck end.

Serves 4

1 chicken, weighing
about 1.5 kg/3 lb

1 small onion, halved

30 g/1 oz/2 tbsp butter, melted

1 tsp ground turmeric

1 tsp ground ginger

1/2 tsp cayenne

salt and pepper

fresh coriander (cilantro),
to garnish

STUFFING

2 tbsp oil

1 medium onion, chopped finely

1/2 medium red (bell) pepper,
chopped finely

2 garlic cloves, crushed

125 g/4 oz/1/2 cup basmati rice

350 ml/12 fl oz/1 1/2 cups
hot chicken stock

grated rind 1/2 lemon

1/2 tsp ground turmeric

1/2 tsp ground ginger

1/2 tsp ground coriander

pinch cayenne pepper

90 g/3 oz/1/2 cup salted cashew
nuts, a little chopped pepper

1 To make the stuffing, heat the oil in a saucepan, add the onion, red pepper and garlic and cook gently for 4–5 minutes. Add the rice and stir to coat with the oil. Add the stock, bring to the boil, then simmer for 15 minutes until all the liquid is absorbed. Transfer to a bowl and add the remaining ingredients for the stuffing. Season well with pepper.

2 Place half the stuffing in the neck end of the chicken and secure with a cocktail stick. Put the halved onion into the cavity of the chicken.

3 Spoon the rest of the rice stuffing into a greased ovenproof dish and cover with foil.

4 Place the chicken in a roasting tin. Prick all over avoiding the stuffed area. Mix the butter and spices, season, then brush over the chicken.

5 Roast in a preheated oven, 190°C/375°F/Gas Mark 5, for 1 hour, basting from time to time. Place the dish of rice stuffing in the oven and continue to cook the chicken for another 30 minutes. Remove the cocktail stick and serve the chicken with stuffing and gravy.

Mexican Chicken

Chilli, tomatoes and corn are typical ingredients
in a Mexican dish.

Serves 4
2 tbsp oil
8 chicken drumsticks
1 medium onion, finely chopped
1 tsp chilli powder
1 tsp ground coriander
425 g/14 oz can chopped tomatoes
2 tbsp tomato purée (paste)
125 g/4 oz/²⁄₃ cup frozen sweetcorn (corn-on-the-cob)
salt and pepper

1 Heat the oil in a large frying pan, add the chicken drumsticks and cook over a medium heat until lightly browned. Remove from the pan and set aside.

2 Add the onion to the pan and cook for 3–4 minutes until soft, then stir in the chilli powder and coriander and cook for a few seconds. Add the chopped tomatoes with their juice and the tomato purée (paste).

3 Return the chicken to the pan and simmer gently for 20 minutes until the chicken is tender and thoroughly cooked. Add the sweetcorn (corn-on-the-cob) and cook a further 3–4 minutes. Season to taste.

4 Serve with rice and mixed (bell) pepper salad.

Golden Chicken Pilau

This is a simple version of a creamy textured and mildly spiced Indian pilau. Although there are lots of ingredients, there's very little preparation needed for this dish.

Serves 4
60 g/2 oz/4 tbsp butter
8 skinless, boneless chicken thighs, cut into large pieces
1 medium onion, sliced
1 tsp ground turmeric
1tsp ground cinnamon
250 g/8 oz/1 cup long grain rice
450 ml/³/₄ pint/1³/₄ cups natural yogurt
60 g/2 oz/¹/₃ cup sultanas
200 ml/7 fl oz/1 scant cup stock
1 medium tomato, chopped
2 tbsp chopped fresh coriander (cilantro) or parsley
2 tbsp toasted coconut
salt and pepper
fresh coriander (cilantro), to garnish

1 Heat the butter in a heavy or non-stick pan and fry the chicken with the onion for about 3 minutes.

2 Stir in the turmeric, cinnamon, rice and seasoning and fry gently for 3 minutes.

3 Add the yogurt, sultanas and stock and mix well. Cover and simmer for 10 minutes, stirring occasionally until the rice is tender and the stock has all been absorbed.

4 Add the tomato and coriander (cilantro) to the pilau. Sprinkle with the toasted coconut and garnish with fresh coriander (cilantro).

Chilli Coconut Chicken

This tasty Thai-style dish has a classic sauce of lime, peanut, coconut and chilli.
You'll find coconut cream in most supermarkets or delicatessens.

Serves 4
30 g/1 oz/$^1/_3$ cup coconut cream
150 ml/$^1/_4$ pint/$^2/_3$ cup hot chicken stock
1 tbsp sunflower oil
8 skinless, boneless chicken thighs, cut into long, thin strips
1 small red chilli, sliced thinly
4 spring onions (scallions), sliced thinly
4 tbsp smooth or crunchy peanut butter
finely grated rind and juice of 1 lime
2 tbsp chopped fresh coriander (cilantro) (optional)

1 Dissolve the coconut cream in the chicken stock.

2 Heat the oil in a wok or large heavy pan and fry the chicken, stirring, until golden. Stir in the chilli and onions and cook gently for a few minutes.

3 Add the peanut butter, coconut cream, lime rind and juice and simmer uncovered, stirring, for about 5 minutes. Serve with boiled rice and sprinkle with coriander (cilantro), if using.

COOK'S VARIATION

Serve jasmine rice with this spicy dish. It has a fragrant aroma that is well-suited to Thai-style recipes.

Chicken in Red (Bell) Pepper & Almond Sauce

This tasty chicken dish combines warm spices and almonds
and is spiked with anise.

Serves 4
30 g/1 oz/2 tbsp butter
7 tbsp vegetable oil
4 skinless, boneless chicken breasts, cut into 4cm/2 inch x 2 cm/1 inch pieces
1 medium onion, roughly chopped
2 cm/1 inch piece fresh ginger root
3 garlic cloves, peeled
30 g/1 oz/¼ cup blanched almonds
1 large red (bell) pepper, roughly chopped
1 tbsp ground cumin
2 tsp ground coriander
1 tsp ground turmeric
pinch cayenne pepper
½ tsp salt
150 ml/¼ pint/⅔ cup water
3 star anise
2 tbsp lemon juice
pepper

4 Add the chicken pieces, the water, star anise, lemon juice and pepper. Cover, reduce the heat and simmer gently for 25 minutes or until the chicken is tender. Stir a few times during cooking.

1 Heat the butter and 1 tablespoon of oil in a frying pan, add the chicken pieces and cook for 5 minutes. Transfer the chicken to a plate.

2 Combine the onion, ginger, garlic, almonds, red pepper, cumin, coriander, turmeric, cayenne and salt in a food processor or liquidiser. Blend to a smooth paste.

3 Heat the remaining oil in a large saucepan or deep frying pan. Add the paste and fry for 10–12 minutes.

Caribbean Chicken

This exotic dish can be made with any cut of chicken, but drumsticks are an
ideal size for quick and even cooking. Coarsely shredded coconut, or even better,
grated fresh coconut, adds a delicious, tropical flavour.

Serves 4
8 skinless chicken drumsticks
2 limes
1 tsp cayenne pepper
2 medium mangoes
1 tbsp sunflower oil
2 tbsp dark muscovado sugar
2 tbsp coarsely grated coconut (optional), to serve

1 With a sharp knife, slash the
chicken drumsticks at intervals then
place the chicken in a large bowl.
Grate the rind from the limes and
set aside.

2 Squeeze the juice from the limes
and sprinkle over the chicken with
the cayenne pepper. Cover and chill
for at least two hours or overnight.

3 Peel and slice the mangoes,
discarding the stone.

4 Drain the chicken drumsticks,
reserving the juice. Heat the oil in a
wide heavy pan and sauté the
chicken, turning frequently, until
golden. Stir in the marinade, lime
rind, mango slices and the sugar.

5 Cover and simmer gently, stirring
occasionally, for 15 minutes, or until
the chicken juices run clear when
pierced with a skewer. Serve
sprinkled with coconut, if using.

Cajun Chicken Gumbo

This complete main course is cooked in one saucepan for simplicity. If you're cooking for one, simply halve the ingredients; the cooking time should stay the same. The whole chilli makes the dish hot and spicy – if you prefer a milder flavour, discard the seeds of the chilli.

Serves 2
1 tbsp sunflower oil
4 chicken thighs
1 small onion, diced
2 sticks (stalks) celery, diced
1 small green (bell) pepper, diced
90 g/3 oz/$\frac{1}{2}$ cup long grain rice
300 ml/$\frac{1}{2}$ pint/$1\frac{1}{4}$ cups chicken stock
1 small red chilli
250 g/8 oz okra
15ml/1 tbsp tomato purée (paste)
salt and pepper

1 Heat the oil in a wide pan and fry the chicken until golden. Remove the chicken from the pan. Stir in the onion, celery and pepper and fry for 1 minute. Pour off any excess fat.

2 Add the rice and fry, stirring for a further minute. Add the stock and heat until boiling.

3 Thinly slice the chilli and trim the okra. Add to the pan with the tomato purée (paste). Season to taste.

4 Return the chicken to the pan and stir. Cover tightly and simmer gently for 15 minutes, or until the rice is tender, the chicken is thoroughly cooked and the liquid absorbed. Stir occasionally and if it becomes too dry, add a little extra stock to moisten.

Cumin Spiced Apricot Chicken

Spiced chicken legs are partially boned and packed with dried apricots for an intense fruity flavour. A golden, spiced, low-fat yogurt coating keeps the chicken moist and tender.

Serves 4
4 large, skinless chicken leg quarters
finely grated rind of 1 lemon
200 g/7 oz/1 cup ready-to-eat dried apricots
1 tbsp ground cumin
1 tsp ground turmeric
125 g/4 oz/½ cup low-fat natural yogurt
salt and pepper

TO SERVE

250 g/8 oz/1½ cups brown rice
2 tbsp flaked hazelnuts or almonds, toasted
2 tbsp sunflower seeds, toasted

1 Remove any excess fat from the chicken legs. Use a small sharp knife to carefully cut the flesh away from the thigh bone.

2 Scrape the meat away down as far as the knuckle. Grasp the thigh bone firmly and twist it to break it away from the drumstick.

3 Open out the boned part of the chicken and sprinkle with lemon rind and pepper. Pack the dried apricots into each piece of chicken.

4 Fold over to enclose, and secure with cocktail sticks. Mix together the cumin, turmeric, yogurt and salt and pepper, then brush this mixture over the chicken to coat evenly. Place the chicken in an ovenproof dish or roasting tin (pan) and bake in a preheated oven, 190°C/375°F/Gas Mark 5, for 35–40 minutes, or until the chicken juices run clear, not pink, when pierced through the thickest part with a skewer.

5 Meanwhile, cook the rice in boiling, lightly salted water until just tender, then drain well. Stir the hazelnuts and sunflower seeds into the rice and serve with the chicken.

Chicken with Peppers & Black Bean Sauce

This tasty chicken stir-fry is quick and easy to make and
is full of fresh flavours and crunchy vegetables.

Serves 4
425 g/14 oz chicken breasts, sliced thinly
pinch of cornflour
2 tbsp oil
1 garlic clove, crushed
1 tbsp black bean sauce
1 each small red and green (bell) pepper, cut into strips
1 red chilli, chopped finely
75 g/3 oz/1 cup mushrooms, sliced
1 onion, chopped
6 spring onions (scallions), chopped
salt and pepper

SEASONING

¹/₂ tsp salt
¹/₂ tsp sugar
3 tbsp chicken stock
1 tbsp dark soy sauce
2 tbsp beef stock
2 tbsp rice wine
1 tsp cornflour, blended with a little rice wine

1 Put the chicken strips in a bowl.
Add a pinch of salt and a pinch of
cornflour and cover with water. Leave
to stand for 30 minutes.

2 Heat 1 tablespoon of the oil in a
wok or deep-sided frying pan and stir-
fry the chicken for 4 minutes. Remove
the chicken to a warm serving dish
and clean the wok or pan.

3 Add the remaining oil to the wok
and add the garlic, black bean sauce,
green and red (bell) peppers, chilli,
mushrooms, onion and spring onions.

Stir fry for 2 minutes then return the
chicken to the wok.

4 Add the seasoning ingredients, fry
for 3 minutes and thicken with a little
cornflour. Serve with fresh noodles.

COOK'S TIP

Black bean sauce can be found in
specialist shops and in many
supermarkets. Use dried noodles if
you can't find fresh noodles.

Thai Stir-Fried Chicken with Vegetables

Coconut adds a creamy texture and delicious flavour to this Thai-style stir-fry, which is spiked with green chilli.

Serves 4
3 tbsp sesame oil
350 g/12 oz chicken breast, sliced thinly
8 shallots, sliced
2 garlic cloves, finely chopped
2.5cm/1 inch piece fresh root ginger, grated
1 green chilli, finely chopped
1 each red and green (bell) pepper, sliced thinly
3 courgettes (zucchini), thinly sliced
2 tbsp ground almonds
1 tsp ground cinnamon
1 tbsp oyster sauce
50 g/2 oz/¼ cup creamed coconut, grated
salt and pepper

1 Heat the sesame oil in a wok, add the chicken, season, and stir fry for about 4 minutes.

2 Add the shallots, garlic, ginger and chilli and stir-fry for 2 minutes.

3 Add the (bell) peppers and courgettes (zucchini) and cook for about 1 minute.

4 Finally, add the ground almonds, cinnamon, oyster sauce and coconut. Stir fry for 1 minute and serve immediately.

Chicken Korma

Korma is a typically mild and aromatic curry. If you want to reduce the fat
in this recipe, use natural yogurt instead of the cream.

Serves 4–6

750 g/1½ lb chicken meat,
cut into cubes

300 ml/½ pint/1¼ cups double
(heavy) cream

½ tsp garam masala

KORMA PASTE

2 garlic cloves

2.5cm/1 inch fresh ginger root,
coarsely chopped

50 g/2 oz/⅓ cup blanched almonds

6 tbsp chicken stock

1 tsp ground cardomon

4 cloves, crushed

1 tsp cinnamon

2 large onions, chopped

1 tsp coriander seeds

2 tsp ground cumin seeds

pinch cayenne

6 tbsp olive oil

salt and pepper

coriander (cilantro), to garnish

1 Place all the ingredients for the korma paste into a blender or food processor and blend together until a very smooth paste is formed.

2 Coat the chicken with the korma paste and chill for 3 hours. Simmer the meat in a large saucepan, adding a little chicken stock if dry.

3 Simmer for 25 minutes, add the cream and garam masala and simmer for a further 15 minutes. Allow the korma to stand for 10 minutes before serving with rice. Garnish with coriander (cilantro).

Fruity Garlic Curried Chicken

Serve this fruity curry with mango chutney and naan bread, and top the curry with seedless grapes. Mango or pears make a good substitute for pineapple.

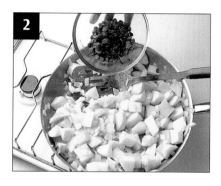

Serves 4–6
1 tbsp oil
900 g/1³/₄ lb chicken meat, chopped
60 g/2 oz/4 tbsp flour, seasoned
32 shallots, roughly chopped
4 garlic cloves, crushed with a little olive oil
3 cooking apples, diced
1 pineapple, diced
125 g/4 oz/³/₄ cup sultanas (golden raisins)
1 tbsp clear honey
300 ml/¹/₂ pint/1¹/₄ cups chicken stock
2 tbsp Worcestershire sauce
3 tbsp hot curry paste
150 ml/¹/₄ pint/²/₃ cup soured cream
salt and pepper

1 Heat the oil in a large frying pan. Coat the meat in the seasoned flour and cook for about 4 minutes until it is browned all over. Transfer the chicken to a large deep casserole.

2 Slowly fry the shallots, garlic, apples, pineapple and sultanas (golden raisins) in the pan juices.

3 Add the chicken stock, seasoning, Worcestershire sauce and curry paste.

4 Pour the sauce over the chicken and cover the casserole with a lid or cooking foil.

5 Cook in the centre of a preheated oven, 180°C/350°F/Gas Mark 4, for 2 hours. Stir in the soured cream and cook for a further 15 minutes. Serve with rice.

Index

Index compiled by Hilary Bird.